The *H*allelujah Diet Workbook

EXPERIENCE *the* OPTIMAL HEALTH YOU WERE MEANT TO HAVE

The *Hallelujah* Diet Workbook

EXPERIENCE *the* OPTIMAL HEALTH YOU WERE MEANT TO HAVE

DR. GEORGE MALKMUS
with PETER & STOWE SHOCKEY

DESTINY IMAGE® PUBLISHERS, INC.

P.O. Box 310, Shippensburg, PA 17257-0310

*"Speaking to the Purposes of God for this Generation
and for the Generations to Come."*

This book and all other Destiny Image, Revival Press, Mercy Place, Fresh Bread, Destiny Image Fiction, and Treasure House books are available at Christian bookstores and distributors worldwide.

For a U.S. bookstore nearest you, call 1-800-722-6774.
For more information on foreign distributors, call 717-532-3040.
Or reach us on the Internet: www.destinyimage.com

ISBN 10: 0-7684-2392-9
ISBN 13: 978-0-7684-2392-1

For Worldwide Distribution, Printed in the U.S.A.

1 2 3 4 5 6 7 8 9 10 11 / 09 08 07 06

The nutritional and health information in this book is based on the teachings of God's Holy Word, the Bible, as well as research and personal experiences by the authors and many others. The purpose of this book is to provide information and education about health. The authors and publisher do not offer medical advice or prescribe the use of diet as a form of treatment for sickness.

Because there is always some risk involved when changing diet and lifestyles, the author and publisher are not responsible for any adverse effects or consequences that might result. Please do not apply the teachings of this book if you are not willing to assume the risk. If you do use the information contained in this book without the approval of a health professional, you are prescribing for yourself, which is your constitutional right, but the author and publisher assume no responsibility.

Contents

CONTENTS

Preface

Welcome, friend! We want to congratulate you for taking the first major step to wonderful health. By deciding to study *The Hallelujah Diet*, you have chosen to drag some of your most unconscious habits out of the shadows and into the light, and thereby into your conscious control. In doing so, you have taken charge of some of the primary factors that determine the condition of your own health—the habitual eating choices that have up to now either promoted life and vitality in your body, or have promoted disease and ill health.

Lifestyle habits are usually based on the buddy system. Think about the lifestyle choices you made in the past—either good or bad—that impact your health now. Maybe it was a bad habit like smoking, drinking, or binging on junk food that led to an unhealthy chapter of your life. Wasn't there someone with whom you tried and then sustained that practice until it became a habit? Or, how about a great sport or exercise routine that improved your health and physique? Odds are, you had someone to play or work out with—a buddy system that helped you both until the activity became part of your lives. Most habits are acquired socially, by the mutual agreement of more than one person.

This workbook provides a connection to a kind of buddy system, whether you are using it in a group or for your own private study. It was designed by people who have been through the program, who understand the ups and downs—and the rewards. While you are reading *The Hallelujah Diet* book, there will be opportunities for you to give feedback and answer questions. You'll be able to express your own goals, and explore your motivations. You'll be examining your own current eating habits, and discussing where those habits came from. Along the way, you'll probably discover that many other people face the same problems you do. And you'll hear how tens of thousands have overcome similar problems, achieving outstanding health and abundant energy.

From all of your friends at Hallelujah Acres we pray that: God blesses our time together; you achieve your goals of optimal health; and, your energy goes through the roof!

How To Use This Study Guide

This study guide is divided into a 12-week program. If you wish to read *The Hallelujah Diet* first, and then review it at the slower pace of this workbook, we encourage you to do so.

And for those who are joining a study group, or simply wishing to absorb the information while getting started on the diet, the job of this book is to *slow down* your reading so you can digest the information packed within gradually—a few chapters at a time. You will not be reading *The Hallelujah Diet* in chronological order. Instead, we have arranged a special weekly sequence—allowing you read along two parallel tracks at once, each week focusing on a particular theme. These two tracks will allow you to gain information (Part One), while at the same time to begin practicing the diet (Part Two).

Parts One and Two are to be used together. Think of Part One (Study Guide) as *information* to help you learn the concepts, and Part Two (Journal) as *interaction* to help you put the concepts into practice. Each weekly section of the Study Guide requires you to read the suggested chapters from *The Hallelujah Diet*, and then asks you to answer several questions in the pages provided. Also, each weekly section of the Journal will give an opportunity to keep records on your health and dietary progress. Each week's assignment is divided into those two parts, each with its own purpose and various written exercises:

Part One - Study Guide. The Study Guide is designed to help you probe deeply into the text of the Hallelujah Diet, and extract the greatest benefit from the information. Part One contains several sections:

Reading Assignments: Reading selections to prepare you for the week's program.

Fact-Finder Questions: Will help you find the nuggets and gems in the week's reading.

Points to Ponder: Help you think about the implications for your life.

Prayer & Reflection: Offers a time for prayer and reflection.

Highlights from Reading: Focus on the key points from the week's selections.

Tips & Quotable Quotes: Tidbits of information, practical suggestions, and wisdom from trusted sources.

Part Two - Journal. The Journal is designed to get you involved interactively by stating your goals, charting your course, and then keeping track of your progress on the Hallelujah Diet. Part Two walks you through a sensible series of steps to get you started on the right foot:

Choices & Goals: Helps you identify and write down your *obstacles* to perfect health; the *consequences* if you don't address those problems; your ultimate health *goals*; and, your deepest reasons for sticking with them.

Charting the Course: Will help you choose which course is right for you.

Journal Entries: Each day you will be required to keep track of your dietary habits. We strongly urge you to make the commitment to journal every day—for the purpose of getting your eating habits out of your unconscious and into your conscious mind.

Your Own Hallelujah Success Story: An opportunity to look back and write your own dramatic results.

Potluck Meal: The final week features a delicious potluck supper for you and your friends!

We have designed the Study Guide and the Journal with the assumption that readers are willing and ready to jump right in—so let's begin!

WEEK 1

I have set before you life and death, blessing and cursing: therefore choose life, that both thou and thy seed may live.
—Deuteronomy 30:19

Die young—as late in life as possible.—Ancient Greek proverb

Welcome to the Hallelujah Diet! Within these pages there is an opportunity to put into practice all the wonderful information and inspiring testimonies that you have either read or are about to read. Make no mistake; you have been led to this moment in time. The doors are about to open. So take a deep breath. You, my friend, are on the threshold of an exciting future—a new you. We're excited for you!

It is our hope that the stories and information shared in *The Hallelujah Diet* book, along with your prayers and ours, will bring about incredible changes in your life and in the lives of those you love.

Before beginning, please be sure you've read How To Use This Study Guide, in the preface of this workbook.

WEEK 1 ASSIGNMENT

    A. Read from *The Hallelujah Diet*:
           Forewords—Page 23
           Preface—Page 27
           Introduction—Page 35

    B. Follow Part One—Study Guide, addressing all questions and activities.

    C. Begin Part Two—Journal for Week 1

PART ONE—STUDY GUIDE

Fact-Finder Questions

1. Through what route of research did Dr. T. Colin Campbell come to conclusions similar to those of Dr. George Malkmus?

_____

_____.

(Answer on page 24.)

2. Is the nutritional content of food—such as those found on product labels—really based on "stable numbers," no matter what methods are used for processing or cooking that food? Yes_____. No_____. I'm not sure_____.
(Answer on page 24.)

3. Research scientists, like those working for drug research companies, food manufacturers, or genetic engineering firms "too often lose sight of the larger contexts that surround these discoveries—like the connections between _____, _____ and _____."
(Answer on page 24.)

4. Vegetable juice as used throughout this book refers to a combination of approximately two-thirds freshly squeezed_____ juice and one-third _____ juice, _____, or _____.
OR: Juice made of 100 percent pure _____ juice is acceptable if desired.
(Answer on page 32.)

5. What primary verse in the Bible is the Hallelujah Diet founded upon? _____.
(Answer on page 35.)

6. What did Daniel ask the supervisor of the Babylonian king's kitchen to feed the youths of Israel for their ten days of dietary testing? _____ to eat, and _____ to drink.
(Answer on page 38.)

7. In which period of history did modern science begin to ignore God as the intelligent designer of the universe, tending from then on to subdue nature rather than to work with it? The

____ ___ _____.

(Answer on page 37.)

8. Most medical schools in the United States require how many classes in nutrition before certifying a doctor to practice medicine?

       A. Six classes.

       B. Three classes.

       C. One class.

       D. No classes.

(Answer on page 39.)

9. You will be seeing the initials or acronym SAD throughout this book. What does it stand for? _____ _____ _____. (Answer on page 38.)

Points to Ponder

1. The Foreword, written by renowned research scientist Dr. T. Colin Campbell, says, "I do not like isolating details from [the] natural order as if they could operate in isolation, especially for commercial purposes. This would violate what I see as an awesome natural biological order, one that is more highly organized, integrated, and controlled than we mere humans could ever duplicate." What do you think these ideas suggest about how research scientists often view nutrition, health, and medicine?

2. When you read the story in the preface about the woman who came to hear about *The Hallelujah Diet* at exactly the right moment, what did you think was actually happening? Do you feel God ever speaks to people in unusual or even miraculous ways? If you know one, give an example:

3. Sometimes the Lord gives us a "feeling" or an intuition to either seek out-or sometimes to avoid-things that will affect our health or well-being. If we decide to ignore God's small voice and go our own way, it can become harder to hear the next time. Can you remember ever having a "bad feeling" the first time you tried something you knew to be unhealthy? What happened to that sense after repeated experiences? Give an example:

4. The book's introduction tells about God's first instruction to humanity: *And God said, Behold, I have given you every herb bearing seed, which is upon the face of all the earth, and every tree, in which is the fruit of a tree yielding seed; to you it shall be for meat* [food] (Genesis 1:29). Over time, humanity has apparently strayed far away from that simple vegetarian diet. Do you see that after many generations, society has completely stopped listening to the inner voice of God regarding healthy eating habits? Name a few examples of things people consume—knowing they are destructive—yet indulge in anyway:

Prayer & Reflection

Take a few moments to pray and reflect upon what you are studying. Here are a few prayer suggestions you may wish to add to your own:

Think about what you can do to improve your own health.

Ask to receive wisdom from the Spirit of Truth—to give discernment about the new ideas presented here.

Learn to understand the difference between appetites based on addictions or sensory pleasures, and appetites based on the healthy instincts designed in us.

Ask for forgiveness for ignoring your own better judgment in the past, and adopting bad habits that may have degraded the physical body—the Temple of the Holy Spirit.

Ask for new and hopeful eyes to see ways of reversing damage done by poor eating habits.

Give thanks and have gratitude for hope in a life free from sickness and fatigue.

Highlights from Reading

God created powerful systems of immunity and self-healing within our bodies—more perfect than science can ever synthesize. But for those systems to be fueled properly, we must willfully put the right elements into our mouths. Does anyone really believe we get sick from a deficiency of drugs? No, we get sick from a deficiency of the vital nutrients God meant for us to eat. But we live in a civilization that gives practically no attention to healthy eating. We mostly follow our lower nature and succumb to our naive and childish appetites.

Over 30 years ago, I was faced with a choice not much different from Daniel's (as a captive of the king of Babylon). I found myself a captive in my own sickened body. Attacked by cancer, I sought the Lord's wisdom. I made the choice to refuse the *king's food*—or what I refer to as the Standard American Diet (SAD)—where we eat like kings at wholesale prices. Instead, I trusted the

God-given mechanisms in my body to heal me, if I supplied the proper nourishment of fresh vegetables and pure water.

I, like Daniel followed what is often called the Genesis 1:29 Diet. I want to repeat that Scripture in which God said to Adam and Eve: *"...I have given you every herb bearing? seed, which is upon the face of all the earth, and every tree, with fruit yielding seed; to you it shall be for meat* [food]."

After all these years of research and experience, my conclusion is that *we do not have to be sick!* Disease and sickness are almost always self—inflicted! Almost every physical problem (other than accidents) is *caused* by improper diet and lifestyle. All we have to do to be well is eat and live according to the way God intended!

If you have taken medications—especially multiple medications on a daily basis—but have felt deep down that it's an expensive and unnatural course to take, get ready to find out why you feel that way. *"And be not conformed to this world: but be ye transformed by the renewing of your mind, that ye may prove what is that good, and acceptable, and perfect, will of God"* (Romans 12:2).

Over the years, we have received thousands of testimonies from people who have switched from the world's way of eating and treating physical problems to God's way. Although our ministry has not always been easy, and we have often faced resistance to this revolutionary message, there has been one thing that drives me on year after year: hearing the *success stories* from people who have regained their health after adopting the Hallelujah Diet!

Tips &
Quotable Quotes

> "The doctor of the future will give no medicine but will interest his patients in the care of the human frame in diet and in the cause and prevention of disease." Thomas A. Edison

> A hot beverage first thing in the morning is good for getting one's bowels moving. As an alternative to caffeine

beverages, try an herbal tea or lemon juice in hot water. Dr. Malkmus

"When you see the Golden Arches, you're probably on the road to the pearly gates." William Castelli, M.D., Director, Framingham Health Study

PART TWO—JOURNAL

Day One:
Your Dietary "Before Picture"

We suggest you fill out several charts—for your own records—at the very beginning of this program. This is very important! It will be a snapshot, a *Before Picture* of your current condition, a kind of health diary. This first week we will concentrate on your *current eating habits*, honestly logging what goes through your mouth and into your body in a typical week. Next week you'll be provided other charts to record the health problems or *obstacles* you face, and your health *goals*. Together these will complete your *Before Picture*, in terms of how your diet affects your health. In 12 weeks, it may be a great surprise for you to look back and see how your overall health has been affected by your changes in diet and lifestyle.

Now, let's analyze your own current eating habits, focusing on three specific categories of food:

List A: SAD Foods — The abbreviation for the *Standard American Diet*. These are foods that are either devoid of nutritional value, improper for our species, or tainted with toxins.

List B: Living Foods — The raw, unprocessed fruits, vegetables, seeds, and nuts that comprise the most healthy and nutritious portion of your diet.

List C: Cooked Foods — These are the kinds of healthy cooked foods that, when taken with a balanced diet of living foods, create a superior nutritional plan.

At the end of List C is a space for a Weekly Reading: "How Do I Feel?" Make a brief note about any changes you may be aware of, including energy boosts or detox reactions.

NOTE: For more details about these three categories of food, please turn to pages 37-39 in this workbook. If you would like more room to write, you can download full sized 8.5 x 11 charts (in PDF format) from our Website at www.hallelujahdietbook.com. Look for appendixes C, D, and E.

WEEKLY JOURNAL: STARTING POINT		
LIST A: SAD FOOD LIST & JOURNAL		
Look at the list on the right. Try to approximate as honestly as possible the **servings and quantities** of the **SAD foods** you consume regularly. Below, write down the foods from the SAD list that you eat in an average week.	Beverages	Alcohol, coffee, tea, cocoa, carbonated beverages and soft drinks, all artificial fruit drinks (including sports drinks), all commercial juices containing preservatives, refined salt, sweeteners.
WEEKLY JOURNAL	Dairy	All animal-based milk, cheese, eggs, ice cream, whipped toppings, non-dairy creamers.
	Fruits	Canned and sweetened fruits, as well as non-organic dried fruits.
	Grains	Refined, bleached-flour products, cold breakfast cereals, white rice.
	Meats	Beef, pork, fish, chicken, turkey, hamburgers, hot dogs, bacon, sausage, etc.
	Nuts/Seeds	All roasted and/or salted seeds, nuts.
	Oils	All lard, margarine, shortenings; anything containing hydrogenated oils.
	Seasonings	Refined table salt, black pepper, any seasonings containing them.
	Soups	All canned or packaged soups, creamed soups that contain dairy products.
	Sweets	All refined white or brown sugar, sugar syrups, chocolate, candy, gum, cookies, donuts, cakes, pies, other products containing refined sugars or artificial sweeteners.
	Vegetables	All canned vegetables with added preservatives or vegetables fried in oil.

Table 1

WEEKLY JOURNAL: Starting Point		
List B: Living Food List & Journal		
Look at the list on the right. Try to approximate the **servings and quantities** of **living foods** you consume regularly. Below, write down the foods from the Living Foods list that you eat in one week.	Beverages	Freshly extracted vegetable juices; BarleyMax, CarrotJuiceMax, BeetMax, distilled water.
Weekly Journal	Dairy Alternatives	Fresh milk derived from oats, rice, coconut, nuts such as almond and hazelnut. Also, "fruit creams" made from strawberry, banana, blueberry.
	Fruits	All fresh, as well as organic "unsulphered" dried fruit.
	Grains	Soaked oats, millet, raw muesli, dehydrated granola or crackers, raw ground flaxseed.
	Beans	Green beans, peas, sprouted garbanzo beans, sprouted lentils, sprouted mung.
	Nuts/Seeds	Raw almonds, sunflower seeds, macadamia nuts, walnuts, raw almond butter, tahini.
	Oils and Fats	Extra virgin olive oil, grapeseed oil for cooking, Udo's Choice Perfected Oil Blend, flaxseed oil, avocados.
	Seasonings	Fresh and dehydrated herbs, garlic, sweet onions, parsley, salt-free seasonings.
	Soups	Raw soups.
	Sweets	Fruit smoothies, raw fruit pies with date/nut crusts, date/nut squares.
	Vegetables	All raw vegetables.

Table 2

WEEKLY JOURNAL: STARTING POINT		
LIST C: COOKED FOOD LIST & JOURNAL		
Look at the list on the right. Try to approximate the **servings and quantities** of healthy **cooked foods** you consume regularly. Below, write down the foods from the Cooked Foods list that you eat in one week.	Beverages	Caffeine-free herb teas, cereal-based coffee beverages, bottled organic juices.
WEEKLY JOURNAL	Dairy Alternatives	Non-dairy cheese and milk, almond milk, nut butters.
	Fruits	Stewed/frozen unsweetened fruits.
	Grains	Whole grain cereals, breads, muffins, pasta, brown rice, spelt, amaranth, millet, etc.
	Beans	Lima, adzuki, black, kidney, navy, pinto, red, white, and other dried beans.
	Oils and Fats	Mayonnaise made from cold-pressed oils, grapeseed oil for cooking.
	Seasonings	Light gray unrefined sea salt, cayenne pepper, all fresh or dried herbs.
	Soups	Soups made from scratch, without fat, dairy, table salt.
	Sweeteners	Raw, unfiltered honey, rice syrup, unsulphered molasses, stevia, carob, pure maple syrup, date sugar.
	Vegetables	Steamed/wok-cooked fresh or frozen vegetables, baked white or sweet potatoes, squash, etc.

Table 3

WEEK 2

Beloved, I wish above all things that thou mayest prosper and be in health, even as thy soul prospereth.—3 John 2

Always bear in mind that your own resolution to success is more important than any other one thing.—Abraham Lincoln (1809-65)

WEEK 2 ASSIGNMENT

A. Read from *The Hallelujah Diet*:
   Chapter One: The Garden Gate—Page 43
   Hallelujah Success Stories: Cancer—Page 67

B. Follow Part One—Study Guide, addressing all questions and activities.

C. Continue with Part Two—Journal for Week 2
   Read Chapter Twenty: Choices & Goals—Page 251
   Complete the Charts.

PART ONE—STUDY GUIDE

Fact-Finder Questions

1. In 1976 Dr. Malkmus was diagnosed with the same illness that had recently taken his own mother's life. What was that illness? _____.
(Answer on page 43.)

2. Lester Roloff—the friend of Dr. Malkmus who first gave him advice about changing his diet—was a professional A) nutritionist B) naturopath C) evangelist D) medical doctor.
(Answer on page 44.)

3. After Dr. Malkmus's baseball-size tumor disappeared as a result of following the Genesis 1:29 Diet, what memorable statement did he make? A) Yippeee! B) Thank heavens I can eat pizza again! C) Hallelujah! D) "Play Ball!"
(Answer on page 45.)

4. How many Americans die of cancer on an average day? _____.
(Answer on page 67.)

5. According to Dr. Neal D. Barnard, president of the Physicians Committee for Responsible Medicine, what kinds of food cause hormonal surges that can trigger the onset of cancer, or make cancer more likely to occur? _____
_____.
(Answer on page 67.)

6. When NASCAR driver Jerrod Sessler's oncologists recommended Interferon and total chemotherapy to slow his advanced melanoma, what results did they predict for him? A) being sick for the next two years B) never having children C) having a short racing career D) all the above.
(Answer on page 69.)

7. Six years after Jerrod Sessler opted for the Hallelujah Diet rather than traditional treatments, the result was: A) total remission within the first year B) three beautiful children C) an ongoing racing career D) all of the above.
(Answer on page 70.)

8. In Rita's story of her cancer treatment, why did she refuse to have her lymph nodes removed? _____

_____.

(Answer on page 71.)

9. Name four types of food in the Standard American Diet (SAD) that are the main culprits of causing cancer. _____, _____, _____, and _____.

(Answer on page 77.)

10. Healing begins with:
      A) Your doctor and taking the proper medications.
      B) Finding a shaman and taking the right potions.
      C) Praying for miracles, and then doing whatever the flesh desires.
      D) Trusting God and being obedient to His natural laws.

(Answer on page 77.)

Points to Ponder

1. As you are gathering your first impressions about the Hallelujah Diet, does it stir up any anxious feelings inside that you will be deprived of some of your favorite things—"the good things in life"? What do you think you might lose?

2. In Chapter One, The Garden Gate, you read about the inner conflict I experienced when I learned I had the same colon cancer that killed my mother. As I was staring death in the face, I was highly motivated to take the advice of my evangelist friend, and try the all-raw food diet. What would it take for you to change your diet and lifestyle in such a profound way?

3. Perhaps you are facing an obstacle to optimum health, like I did with colon cancer. It might be a serious condition like cancer or heart disease, or it might be something less easy to name, like tiredness or just foggy thinking. Can you name any obstacles you are facing that prevent you from enjoying the perfect health God wishes for you, physically, emotionally, and spiritually?

Prayer & Reflection

> Take a few moments to pray and reflect upon what you are studying. Here are a few prayer suggestions you may wish to add to your own:

> If you have previously prayed for a healing miracle and none came, ask why. Was it lack of faith, or a lack of knowledge?

> If you or someone you love is facing a serious illness, ask God for wisdom to know what to do, and whether the source of healing is something that comes from inside or outside of you.

> If the testimonial stories you read seem too good to be true, ask for confirmation to come from a source you know and trust. Reflect deeply on your fundamental understanding about the source of health and healing, and ask God to address any of your lifelong beliefs that might need to be reconsidered.

Highlights from Reading

And then, like the setting of my life's sunshine, she was gone; her suffering finally ended. But in the difficult days that followed I began my own struggle, trying to come to terms with why Mom had to die and why she suffered so much. I knew that many types of cancer were often fatal, but deep down I couldn't shake the feeling that it was the *treatments* she received at the hands of the medical doctors—and not the cancer itself—that ultimately caused her death.

It was during this time of uncertainty that I turned for help to Lester Roloff, an evangelist friend of mine in Texas. Brother Roloff was one of those "health nuts," and we often affectionately referred to him as "Carrot Juice Roloff." I desperately needed someone to talk to, someone who could make some sense out of my situation. I'll admit that his advice made anything but sense at first. In fact, it sounded pretty strange. But the more he talked, the more something inside of me said, *this is right.*

The results were spectacular! Almost immediately, I started to get well! In less than one year, my tumor had totally disappeared. It simply got smaller and smaller until it was gone. But that was not all! In less than one year, every other physical problem I had been experiencing also disappeared! Hemorrhoids, hypoglycemia, severe allergies and sinus problems, high blood pressure, fatigue, pimples, colds, flu—even body odor and dandruff—were gone! *Totally healed!*

After all these years of research and experience, my conclusion is that *we do not have to be sick*! Disease and sickness are almost always self—inflicted! Almost every physical problem (other than accidents) is *caused* by improper diet and lifestyle. All we have to do to be well is eat and live according to the way God intended!

YES! You can keep from getting cancer! Testimonies from around the world prove there is absolutely something you can do to lower your odds of getting this dreaded disease.

The American Cancer Society's annual estimate of new cancer cases and deaths projects 1,372,910 new cancer cases in the United States in 2005 and 570,280 cancer deaths—or about 1,500 a day; that is over a half million people who died from cancer in the United States alone, making it the second leading cause of death after heart disease in this country.

We submit to radiation that will burn a part of our body or surgery to cut out a part of our body—all this in an effort to affect a cure! And to top it off, we are willing to spend all the money we have and all the money we don't have in our search for a miracle cure.

If a doctor administers chemotherapy drugs to a healthy person it makes them sick. So how can we think giving the same toxic drugs to a sick person would make them healthy? It just doesn't make sense. When these invasive techniques are used, the body must divert valuable energy needed for healing the cancer in order to deal with what it sees as a threat to basic survival.

"You know, the best thing I've noticed about living this lifestyle is how much more mental clarity I have. In fact," Jerrod Sessler says, "all my relationships are better—with my Lord, my wife, and my family. I would recommend this lifestyle to anybody!"

Tips &
Quotable Quotes

> You'll have better results breaking old bad habits by replacing them with good new ones. As the 15th century priest Desiderius Erasmus said, "A nail is driven out by another nail. Habit is overcome by habit."

> "One pint of carrot juice, daily, has more constructive body value than 25 pounds of calcium tablets." Dr. Norman W. Walker

> "Five of the ten leading causes of illness and death are associated with diet (coronary heart disease, cancer, stroke, diabetes, and atherosclerosis). It is now clear that diet contributes in substantial ways to the development of these diseases and that modification of diet can contribute to their prevention and control." David DeRose, M.D.

PART TWO—JOURNAL

By the end of Chapter One, a source of great hope is revealed for many people who are needlessly suffering from the ill effects of poor diet. To share that sense of hope in what you have read so far, here's an opportunity to put it into words. The next few pages are provided for you to spell out your *hopes* in a creatively constructive way—in the shape of *Goals*. Be sure you have read Chapter Twenty, Choices & Goals, before you go further.

As you complete the following pages, think about the conditions that might be keeping you from enjoying a life of optimum health and abundant energy.

1. Start by spelling out the *obstacles* you wish to overcome. They might fall into physical, emotional or spiritual obstacles—or perhaps all three.

2. Then spell out the *consequences* you might face if you don't deal with those obstacles. Be realistic. "If I don't lose weight, I could have a heart attack."

3. Next, clearly spell out your *goals*. Be specific about what you want to achieve. The more vividly you can paint the picture of perfect health, the more willpower you will tap to achieve your goals.

4. Finally, give the *reasons* why you wish to achieve your goals. This will help cement your resolution to stick to your guns, even when tempted to give up.

Reminder: After you complete the four charts, don't forget to continue with this week's Journal entry.

Hallelujah Health Goals		
Name:		Date:
Age:	Height:	Weight:

ENERGY LEVEL: On a scale between 1 and 10, (1 is lowest energy and 10 is highest energy), how would you rate your average energy level these days?

_____

I. OBSTACLES: PHYSICAL, EMOTIONAL & SPIRITUAL

Clearly spell out the obstacle(s) you want to address under each category. For example, under "Physical" you might write:
"I am 30 lbs. overweight and suffer from hypertension" or *"I have bad acne and skin rashes"* or *"I am frequently tired and need a nap in the afternoon"* or *"I drink 4 cups of coffee to stay alert while driving."*

Physical

Emotional

Spiritual

Table 4

II. CONSEQUENCES: PHYSICAL, EMOTIONAL & SPIRITUAL
What happens if you don't deal with the obstacle(s)?   For example, under "Physical" you might write,   "*My husband probably doesn't appreciate the extra weight I've put on since we were married, and I don't want him to find me less attractive,*" or "*According to my doctor, I am risking a heart attack, and the only alternative is going on medication which I DON'T WANT to do,*" or "*Although my acne gives me a 'youthful' appearance, I'm ready to face the fact that it's a sign of a poor diet.*"

Physical

Emotional

Spiritual

Table 5

III. GOALS: PHYSICAL, EMOTIONAL & SPIRITUAL

Now that you've stated the obstacles and the consequences, clearly write out your goals regarding what you want to achieve. This should be the *opposite* of the obstacle(s) you listed. Try going beyond the obstacle to create a perfectly healthy new you! For example, under "Physical" you might write,
"*I, Jane Doe, am going to lose 30 lbs. of excess fat and become even more attractive to my husband than when we first met!*" or "*Next time I go to the doctor, I'm going to have a normal blood-pressure reading, and I won't need any drugs,*" or "*My pimples are going to go away, because toxins will be gone from my body.*"

Physical

Emotional

Spiritual

Table 6

IV. REASONS: PHYSICAL, EMOTIONAL & SPIRITUAL
Although "Reasons" may look similar to "Consequences," they are actually the *positive* flipside. For example, under "Physical" you might write, "*I want to be at an ideal weight because I want to glorify God with the ideal body He gave me, overflowing with health and vitality. I also want my heart to be in top condition so that I'm around for my children, and they can look at Mom and say, 'I want to be healthy like her too!'*"

Physical

Emotional

Spiritual

Table 7

JOURNAL FOR WEEK 2—LIST A		
SAD FOODS		
Look at the list on the right. Try to approximate as honestly as possible the **servings and quantities** of the **SAD foods** you consume regularly. Below, write down the foods from the SAD list that you eat in an average week.	Beverages	Alcohol, coffee, tea, cocoa, carbonated beverages and soft drinks, all artificial fruit drinks (including sports drinks), all commercial juices containing preservatives, refined salt, sweeteners.
WEEKLY JOURNAL	Dairy	All animal-based milk, cheese, eggs, ice cream, whipped toppings, non-dairy creamers.
	Fruits	Canned and sweetened fruits, as well as non-organic dried fruits.
	Grains	Refined, bleached-flour products, cold breakfast cereals, white rice.
	Meats	Beef, pork, fish, chicken, turkey, hamburgers, hot dogs, bacon, sausage, etc.
	Nuts/Seeds	All roasted and/or salted seeds, nuts.
	Oils	All lard, margarine, shortenings; anything containing hydrogenated oils.
	Seasonings	Refined table salt, black pepper, any seasonings containing them.
	Soups	All canned or packaged soups, creamed soups that contain dairy products.
	Sweets	All refined white or brown sugar, sugar syrups, chocolate, candy, gum, cookies, donuts, cakes, pies, other products containing refined sugars or artificial sweeteners.
	Vegetables	All canned vegetables with added preservatives or vegetables fried in oil.

Table 8

JOURNAL FOR WEEK 2—LIST B		
LIVING FOODS		
Look at the list on the right. Try to approximate the **servings and quantities** of **living foods** you consume regularly. Below, write down the foods from the Living Foods list that you eat in one week.	Beverages	Freshly extracted vegetable juices (2/3 carrot and 1/3 greens), BarleyMax, CarrotJuiceMax, BeetMax, distilled water.
WEEKLY JOURNAL	Dairy Alternatives	Fresh milk derived from oats, rice, coconut, nuts such as almond and hazelnut. Also, "fruit creams" made from strawberry, banana, blueberry.
	Fruits	All fresh, as well as organic "unsulphered" dried fruit.
	Grains	Soaked oats, millet, raw muesli, dehydrated granola or crackers, raw ground flaxseed.
	Beans	Green beans, peas, sprouted garbanzo beans, sprouted lentils, sprouted mung.
	Nuts/Seeds	Raw almonds, sunflower seeds, macadamia nuts, walnuts, raw almond butter, tahini.
	Oils and Fats	Extra virgin olive oil, grapeseed oil for cooking, Udo's Choice Perfected Oil Blend, flaxseed oil, avocados.
	Seasonings	Fresh and dehydrated herbs, garlic, sweet onions, parsley, salt-free seasonings.
	Soups	Raw soups.
	Sweets	Fruit smoothies, raw fruit pies with date/nut crusts, date/nut squares.
	Vegetables	All raw vegetables.

Table 9

JOURNAL FOR WEEK 2—LIST C		
COOKED FOOD LIST AND JOURNAL		
Look at the list on the right. Try to approximate the **servings and quantities** of healthy **cooked foods** you consume regularly. Below, write down the foods from the Cooked Foods list that you eat in one week.	Beverages	Caffeine-free herb teas, cereal-based coffee beverages, bottled organic juices.
WEEKLY JOURNAL	Dairy Alternatives	Non-dairy cheese and milk, almond milk, nut butters.
	Fruits	Stewed/frozen unsweetened fruits.
	Grains	Whole grain cereals, breads, muffins, pasta, brown rice, spelt, amaranth, millet, etc.
	Beans	Lima, adzuki, black, kidney, navy, pinto, red, white, and other dried beans.
	Oils and Fats	Mayonnaise made from cold-pressed oils, grapeseed oil for cooking.
	Seasonings	Light gray unrefined sea salt, cayenne pepper, all fresh or dried herbs.
	Soups	Soups made from scratch, without fat, dairy, table salt.
	Sweeteners	Raw, unfiltered honey, rice syrup, unsulphered molasses, stevia, carob, pure maple syrup, date sugar.
	Vegetables	Steamed/wok-cooked fresh or frozen vegetables, baked white or sweet potatoes, squash, etc.

Table 10

WEEK 3

And God said, Behold, I have given you every herb bearing seed, which is upon the face of all the earth, and every tree, in which is the fruit of a tree yielding seed; to you it shall be for meat [food].—Genesis 1:29

WEEK 3 ASSIGNMENT

A. Read from *The Hallelujah Diet*:
   Chapter Two: A Biblical Foundation—Page 49
   Hallelujah Success Stories: Osteoporosis and Arthritis—
   Page 99

B. Follow Part One—Study Guide, addressing all questions
   and activities.

C. Part Two—Journal for Week 3
   Read Chapter Twenty-one: Charting the Course—
   Page 255
   Fill out charts.
   Continue writing in your Weekly Journal.

PART ONE—STUDY GUIDE

Fact-Finder Questions

1. *And God said, Let the earth bring forth _____, the _____ yielding _____, and the _____ tree yielding _____ after his kind, whose ____ is in itself, upon the earth: and it was so... and God saw that it was _____* (Genesis 1:11-12). (Answer on page 49.)

2. Write down the Bible verse from Psalm 139:14: _____

_____

_____.

(Answer on page 51.)

3. Whole, raw foods appeal to which of our senses when in their natural unadulterated state? A) sight, B) touch, C) smell, D) taste, E) all the above.
(Answer on page 50.)

4. As we learned in Chapter Two, meats "move very sluggishly through the digestive tract, and in an atmosphere of 98.6 degrees, they putrefy!" Name several physical problems in our bodies that are caused by this rotting food: _____

_____.

(Answer on page 53.)

5. Until the Great Flood, the patriarchs lived an average of how many years while following the diet prescribed in Genesis 1:29? _____.
(Answer on page 52.)

6. What immune-suppressing ingredient does the average American eat 170 pounds of annually? _____.
(Answer on page 54.)

7. One of the greatest reasons we should be taking care of our physical health is because our bodies are the temple of _____. A) Love B) Doom C) Shirley D) the Holy Spirit!
(Answer on page 54.)

8. *Beloved, I wish above all things that thou mayest prosper and be in _____, even as thy soul prospereth* (3 John 2).
(Answer on page 55.)

Points to Ponder

1. What is it that causes people to do what they know to be wrong, and to adopt habits they know are destructive? Read Romans 7:14-20 for some insight on why we naturally make bad choices. Name some bad habits people choose, despite knowing better, that undermine what God wishes for their health and happiness. Now, as honestly as possible, list a few *eating habits* you have acquired in spite of knowing better:

2. When Daniel and his friends were captives in Babylon, they could have easily indulged in food and wine from the king's table, but they made a special effort to resist and were healthier as a result. Sometimes our own civilization is compared to Babylon in its decadent and sensually indulgent ways. Can you name several aspects of life in which a person requires self-control when confronted with temptations from our so-called modern-day Babylon?

3. The instincts that we are created with—together with the natural appreciation for colors, tastes, textures, and aromas—give us clues about what God wants us to eat. Yet somehow our civilization manages to alter and redirect many of our natural appetites and instincts, for the purpose of selling products—a bait and switch strategy. Can you name some foods that often substitute unnatural ingredients to fool our natural senses?

Sweet tastes in fruit: substituted with_____.

Fruity flavors and aromas: substituted with artificial flavors in_____.

Vibrant colors in fruits and vegetables: substituted with artificial colors in _____.

Crunchy textures of natural produce: substituted with _____.

Luscious oils in nuts, seeds, avocados, and similar items: substituted with _____.

Prayer & Reflection

Take a few moments to pray and reflect upon what you are studying. Here are a few prayer suggestions you may wish to add to your own:

What condition does God really wish for my body, as the Temple of the Holy Spirit? Why does it even make a difference?

If we—like the Babylonians in the days of Daniel—have been unknowingly deceived by what our society considers a "normal" diet, then where can we turn to learn what our body was originally designed to eat?

Isn't it enough to pray for miraculous healing when we are sick, rather than get so concerned with what we eat and drink every day?

When it comes to our health where does personal responsibility begin and end?

Highlights from Reading

In Genesis 1:29, God told Adam that these fruits, vegetables, seeds, and nuts in the Garden that He had previously created were to be Adam's food. Who would know better what Adam's physical body had been designed to be nourished with, than the very Creator of that physical body?

However, when an animal source food is consumed, and sent through the digestive tract, a digestive tract that was designed by God to process raw fruits and vegetables loaded with fiber, problems develop! Why? Because animal products contain absolutely no fiber! Thus, animal foods move very sluggishly through the digestive tract, in an atmosphere of 98.6

degrees, and they putrefy! This putrefied flesh causes physical problems that range from body odor to acid stomach problems, to Irritable Bowel Syndrome (IBS), to colitis, to ulcerated colitis, to Crohn's disease, to colon cancer.

Preachers, like myself, dedicate their lives to serving the people in our churches. However, for far too long now we have only ministered to their spiritual needs, while relegating their physical needs to prayer and the world's medical system. Jesus ministered to more than just the peoples' spiritual needs; He also ministered to their physical and emotional needs. In Third John 2, we are told of God's will for His people concerning their physical bodies: *Beloved, I wish above all things that thou mayest prosper and be in health, even as thy soul prospereth.*

Surgery, radiation, chemotherapy, and other drugs are not God's answers to sickness. They are unnatural and interfere with the body's ability to heal itself. Moreover, they simply treat the symptoms and not the disease. The Bible has many instructions about how we are meant to care for our bodies. We must go to the Bible for instruction about our health, rather than to the world.

Dr. Rowen Pfeiffer says, "Many people don't realize that we are one of the highest dairy-consuming countries on the planet, yet we have the highest rate of osteoporosis anywhere. The countries that take in the highest levels of dairy products have the highest levels of osteoporosis. The countries that have the least intake of calcium and dairy products have the least amount of osteoporosis. It's really the high consumption of protein that is the problem."

Many doctors cite a diet high in protein as being one of the main culprits of arthritis. Dr. Rowen Pfeiffer explains, "Your body can only process the uric acid of a very small amount of meat every day—about four ounces. When you're taking in anywhere from 8 to 25 ounces of meat a day, you've got all this uric acid your body cannot eliminate. Then it crystallizes. It's like broken glass. And it tends to settle in your joints, actually shredding the cartilage."

"A lot of people just want to take pills and continue with their lifestyle," says Dr. Rowen Pfeiffer. "But you can't keep creating a problem and then try to take something to undo it. It just doesn't work that way. We have to hit it from both sides. Stop creating the problem, and begin doing the things that will make it heal."

Tips &
Quotable Quotes

"The average supermarket is a mausoleum where dead foods lie in state." Evangelist Lester Roloff

"The best strategy for slowing the aging process is nutrition. We can better the quality of life and prolong our existence by fixing our eyes on nature. That is to say, our food must be eaten as God put it in the world, without alteration." Francisco Contreras, M.D.

"We squander Health
In search of Wealth,
We scheme and toil and save:
Then squander Wealth
In search of Health—
And all we get is a grave"
H.E. Kirschner, M.D.

PART TWO—JOURNAL

Be sure to read Chapter Twenty-one, Charting the Course, before filling out the following chart.

This will be the week when you decide what direction you'll be taking for the next nine weeks.

If you feel the need to jump in with both feet by taking the "Recovery" course—either because you are suffering an illness that needs addressing, or perhaps because you want to achieve optimal health as soon as possible—then follow the instructions on the left side of the chart. Complete the "Agreement with Myself" and turn directly to page 255 in *The Hallelujah Diet* book. Also be sure to read Chapters Ten and Twenty-three in the coming week.

If you feel more inclined to take the "Maintenance" course—transitioning into the various new aspects of the Hallelujah Diet at your own pace—then follow the instructions on the right side of the chart, completing the "Agreement with Myself" before continuing with your Journal.

Then, continue your Journal entries for this week.

CHARTING THE COURSE	
CHOOSE YOUR CORRECT LEVEL	
Recovery	**Maintenance**
If you choose to go "cold turkey," you will need to carefully read Chapters Ten and Twenty-three from *The Hallelujah Diet* book, so you will know how to equip yourself.	If you've chosen to transition more slowly into the Hallelujah Diet, make sure you have spelled out exactly what your typical weekly menu *currently* looks like using the charts in Lists A, B, and C from Week 1.
There is a basic Hallelujah Diet on page 145, in Chapter Ten to help you get started. You will also continue to journal for the remainder of the workbook, after which you can continue to do so as long as you wish until you are comfortable with the new diet and lifestyle.	Then, use the Destination Replacement Journal Chart (Table 22.13, page 360) to spell out the steps you'll take to replace one SAD food habit with one good food habit. We've designed it as a daily transition schedule, but you may wish to convert it to weekly or longer, depending on how quickly you feel you and your family can make the transition.

Table 11

AGREEMENT WITH MYSELF

CHOSEN LEVEL:
(Circle One)
RECOVERY   MAINTENANCE

I, (name) _____ on, (today's date)
_____ am making a commitment to myself and
my loved ones to follow the Hallelujah Diet, at the (chosen
level) _____ level, for a period of time no less
than _____ weeks.

I am aware of the obstacles in my life, which prevent me
from enjoying optimal health, and I am aware of the possible
consequences if I do not overcome those obstacles.

I have clearly spelled out my physical, emotional, and spiritual goals for good health. I will faithfully and honestly keep
track of what I am currently eating in my journal, and then
will continue to track my progress as I transition into the
Hallelujah Diet.

(Additional notes to self)

_____

_____

_____

_____

_____

SIGNED _____

DATED: _____

Table 12

JOURNAL FOR WEEK 3—LIST A		
SAD FOODS		
Look at the list on the right. Try to approximate as honestly as possible the **servings and quantities** of the **SAD foods** you consume regularly. Below, write down the foods from the SAD list that you eat in an average week.	Beverages	Alcohol, coffee, tea, cocoa, carbonated beverages and soft drinks, all artificial fruit drinks (including sports drinks), all commercial juices containing preservatives, refined salt, sweeteners.
WEEKLY JOURNAL	Dairy	All animal-based milk, cheese, eggs, ice cream, whipped toppings, non-dairy creamers.
	Fruits	Canned and sweetened fruits, as well as non-organic dried fruits.
	Grains	Refined, bleached-flour products, cold breakfast cereals, white rice.
	Meats	Beef, pork, fish, chicken, turkey, hamburgers, hot dogs, bacon, sausage, etc.
	Nuts/Seeds	All roasted and/or salted seeds, nuts.
	Oils	All lard, margarine, shortenings; anything containing hydrogenated oils.
	Seasonings	Refined table salt, black pepper, any seasonings containing them.
	Soups	All canned or packaged soups, creamed soups that contain dairy products.
	Sweets	All refined white or brown sugar, sugar syrups, chocolate, candy, gum, cookies, donuts, cakes, pies, other products containing refined sugars or artificial sweeteners.
	Vegetables	All canned vegetables with added preservatives or vegetables fried in oil.

Table 13

JOURNAL FOR WEEK 3—LIST B		
LIVING FOODS		
Look at the list on the right. Try to approximate the **servings and quantities** of **living foods** you consume regularly. Below, write down the foods from the Living Foods list that you eat in one week.	Beverages	Freshly extracted vegetable juices (2/3 carrot and 1/3 greens), BarleyMax, CarrotJuiceMax, BeetMax, distilled water.
WEEKLY JOURNAL	Dairy Alternatives	Fresh milk derived from oats, rice, coconut, nuts such as almond and hazelnut. Also, "fruit creams" made from strawberry, banana, blueberry.
	Fruits	All fresh, as well as organic "unsulphered" dried fruit.
	Grains	Soaked oats, millet, raw muesli, dehydrated granola or crackers, raw ground flaxseed.
	Beans	Green beans, peas, sprouted garbanzo beans, sprouted lentils, sprouted mung.
	Nuts/Seeds	Raw almonds, sunflower seeds, macadamia nuts, walnuts, raw almond butter, tahini.
	Oils and Fats	Extra virgin olive oil, grapeseed oil for cooking, Udo's Choice Perfected Oil Blend, flaxseed oil, avocados.
	Seasonings	Fresh and dehydrated herbs, garlic, sweet onions, parsley, salt-free seasonings.
	Soups	Raw soups.
	Sweets	Fruit smoothies, raw fruit pies with date/nut crusts, date/nut squares.
	Vegetables	All raw vegetables.

Table 14

JOURNAL FOR WEEK 3—LIST C		
HALLELUJAH COOKED FOODS		
Look at the list on the right. Try to approximate the **servings and quantities** of healthy **cooked foods** you consume regularly. Below, write down the foods from the Cooked Foods list that you eat in one week.	Beverages	Caffeine-free herb teas, cereal-based coffee beverages, bottled organic juices.
WEEKLY JOURNAL	Dairy Alternatives	Non-dairy cheese and milk, almond milk, nut butters.
	Fruits	Stewed/frozen unsweetened fruits.
	Grains	Whole grain cereals, breads, muffins, pasta, brown rice, spelt, amaranth, millet, etc.
	Beans	Lima, adzuki, black, kidney, navy, pinto, red, white, and other dried beans.
	Oils and Fats	Mayonnaise made from cold-pressed oils, grapeseed oil for cooking.
	Seasonings	Light gray unrefined sea salt, cayenne pepper, all fresh or dried herbs.
	Soups	Soups made from scratch, without fat, dairy, table salt.
	Sweeteners	Raw, unfiltered honey, rice syrup, unsulphered molasses, stevia, carob, pure maple syrup, date sugar.
	Vegetables	Steamed/wok-cooked fresh or frozen vegetables, baked white or sweet potatoes, squash, etc.

Table 15

WEEK 4

Imagine life as a game in which you are juggling five balls in the air. You name them—work, family, health, friends, and spirit—and you're keeping all of these in the air. You will soon understand that work is a rubber ball. If you drop it, it will bounce back. But the other four balls—family, health, friends, and spirit—are made of glass. If you drop one of these, they will be irrevocably scuffed, marked, nicked, damaged, or even shattered. They will never be the same. You must understand that and strive for balance in your life.
—Brian Dyson, CEO of Coca Cola Enterprises from 1959–1994

WEEK 4 ASSIGNMENT

A. Read from *The Hallelujah Diet*:
   Chapter Three: What Is Life?—Page 57
   Hallelujah Success Stories: Diabetes—Page 131

B. Follow Part One—Study Guide, addressing all questions and activities.

C. Continue with Part Two—Journal for Week 4
   Read Chapter Ten: The Hallelujah Diet Explained—Page 141
   Continue writing in your Journal.

PART ONE—STUDY GUIDE

Fact-Finder Questions

1. According to John 10:10, found in the third paragraph of Chapter Three, what is it that God wants for us? _____

_____

_____.

(Answer on page 57.)

2. According to page 57, how many times is the word *life* found in the Scriptures? _____ The Scriptures are talking not only about spiritual life but also _____life. (Answer on page 61.)

3. According to Dr. Joel Fuhrman, author of *Eat to Live*, with what does the epidemic of diabetes in our country today correspond?_____ _____

_____.

(Answer on page 131.)

4. TRUE or FALSE:
   A) Insulin is like a doorman. T / F
   B) Insulin is made by eating lots of sugary cakes and cookies. T / F
   C) Insulin opens the door of the cell, puts the sugar inside, and closes the door. T / F
   D) Our diets are often so fatty that the doorknob to our cell is too greasy for insulin to open it up. T / F
   E) Eating vegetables and fruits can cause you to have to take more medications such as laxatives. T / F

(Answers on page 132.)

5. Dr. Fuhrman tells us that even minimal _____ _____ can lead to diabetes. (Answer on page 134.)

6. Many times the first symptom of diabetes is a _____ _____.

(Answer on page 133.)

7. Dr. Fuhrman says, "If we had never invented medications to treat diabetes, like insulin and other drugs, maybe then doctors would have been forced to tell people they have to _____
_____!"

(Answer on page 136.)

Points to Ponder

1. Scientists have been unsuccessfully trying to create *life* in the lab for years by combining lifeless, inanimate compounds hoping that *life* will spring fourth. Yet the Bible tells us that God breathed His own Spirit—the breath of *life*—into humans and all living things, and then provided *living* food as a source of energy. How do you think humanity came to believe we can perpetuate life and health in our bodies by the consumption of inanimate, dead foods?

2. My eyesight not only stopped degenerating after adopting the diet of living foods, but the damage was actually reversed and regenerated into 20/20 vision! Most people would be surprised to discover they can slow down the degenerative aging process, but how do you personally react to the idea that living food can actually repair the damage already done? What do you think are the possible implications on the subject of aging?

3. We read that many patients with Type 2 diabetes can often get off insulin injections permanently within 30 days of changing their diet. Many doctors understand this, and yet their patients don't want to hear it because it involves making an effort. This echoes what many doctors agonize about when, for example, heart patients refuse to lose weight, or cancer patients refuse to quit smoking. Why do you suppose people are often more willing to face expensive and drawn out treatments, rather than to make simple changes to their lifestyles?

Prayer & Reflection

Take a few moments to pray and reflect upon what you are studying. Here are a few prayer suggestions you may wish to add to your own:

Ask God why He put *life* into your body—and into the material realm—in the first place.

Pray for a simple example to come to you in the next week; one that illustrates the chain of life transferred from living food into a living, healthy body.

Reflect on the tendency of mankind to twist things that are simple, natural, and glorifying to God, into something distorted.

Pray for God to reveal areas of your life that could be improved to be more like His original designs for them.

Highlights from Reading

I have set before you life and death, blessing and cursing: therefore choose life, that both thou and thy seed may live (Deut. 30:19).

The white milk coming out of a mother's breast is better than a *blood* transfusion to support her baby's *life*. It really is amazing when you think about it.

The longer we stay on the wrong fuel, the louder the pinging and the knocking. If we stay on the wrong fuel long enough, ultimately the pinging and knocking will get extremely loud. When we change the fuel and start putting into our bodies the fuel that God designed as nourishment, our bodies will respond and nearly always correct the physical problem. It can and will heal itself!

For five years, Rhonda and I lived on a mountain farm with deer running all over the property, and we never saw a fat deer! You see, they eat food the way God designed it to be consumed, and consequently they don't have a problem—and neither will we when we start eating the way God designed our bodies to be nourished.

Gary feels this is a lifestyle change that, for him, is worth the effort. "This is the way for me," he says. "It's a God-based diet, and I really believe the God-given principles are the most important principles we can follow. I just thank God for the Hallelujah Diet. I'd recommend it to anyone!"

Dr. Joel Fuhrman, author of *Eat to Live*, says, "We have an epidemic of diabetes in this country today, which corresponds with the increase in obesity. That's because adult onset (or Type 2) diabetes is predominantly a disease of being overweight."

> *Bless the Lord, O my soul, and forget not all his benefits: Who forgiveth all thine iniquities; who healeth all thy diseases; Who redeemeth thy life from destruction; who crowneth thee with lovingkindness and tender mercies; Who satisfieth thy mouth with good things; so that thy youth is renewed like the eagle's* (Psalm 103:2-5).

*Tips &
Quotable Quotes*

> "Only small intakes of animal products were associated with significant increases in chronic degenerative diseases." T. Colin Campbell, The China Project

"Life is like a gun. It can be aimed in only one direction at a time. Make your aim—health!" Paul Bragg

"If mankind would at once discard all refined, sprayed, and unnatural foods, it would be the beginning of a race of people who would live long happy lives and be free of disease." Paul Bragg

Part Two—Journal

First, carefully read Chapter Ten: The Hallelujah Diet Explained. This is perhaps the most important chapter in the entire book in terms of lifesaving and vital information. This is where some people might say, "I can't do that!"—to which I say, "Sure you can, millions have already and lived to tell about it—and many of them wouldn't have lived otherwise!"

This might be a good time to get in touch with your inner child and gently take charge, by saying things like: "You need to eat your broccoli because I love you, and because I say so." Or, "I'm sorry, but those sweets will spoil your appetite for real living foods." The point is, many people have not grown up to the fact that they are 100 percent responsible for their own health—and their food choices have to become a disciplined part of life, just like good hygiene and dressing themselves.

Carefully study the following food charts. Understanding these lists—and identifying the principles behind them—is the key to successfully adopting the Hallelujah Diet into your own life.

After studying the charts, continue your Journal entries for this week.

CATEGORY A—BAD AND SAD FOODS (DEAD FOODS TO AVOID)		
By the time you reach this point in the book, it should be clear how sickness comes from the collection of garbage in our SAD (Standard American Diet). When you have made a commitment to *The Hallelujah Diet*, and to better health, it will be psychologically easier for you to completely eliminate these dead and deadly foods, preventing them from ever entering your body through the gateway of your mouth.		
Beverages	Alcohol, coffee, tea, cocoa, carbonated beverages and soft drinks, all artificial fruit drinks (including sports drinks), all commercial juices containing preservatives, refined salt, sweeteners.	
Dairy	All animal-based milk, cheese, eggs, ice cream, whipped toppings, non-dairy creamers.	
Fruits	Canned and sweetened fruits, as well as non-organic dried fruits.	
Grains	Refined, bleached flour products, cold breakfast cereals, white rice.	
Meats	Beef, pork, fish, chicken, turkey, hamburgers, hot dogs, bacon, sausage, etc.	NOTE: All meats are harmful to the body and are the primary or contributing cause of most physical problems.
Nuts and Seeds	All roasted and/or salted seeds/nuts.	NOTE: Peanuts are legumes and are very difficult to digest.
Oils	All lard, margarine, shortenings; anything containing hydrogenated oils.	
Seasonings	Refined table salt, black pepper, any seasonings containing them.	
Soups	All canned or packaged soups, creamed soups that contain dairy products.	
Sweets	All refined white or brown sugar, sugar syrups, chocolate, candy, gum, cookies, donuts, cakes, pies, other products containing refined sugars or artificial sweeteners.	
Vegetables	All canned vegetables with added pre-preservatives or vegetables fried in oil.	

Table 16

CATEGORY B—HALLELUJAH DIET FOODS–LIVING FOODS TO INCLUDE		
Raw Foods (Ratio: 85%)		
Dense, living nutrients are found in raw (uncooked), natural, unprocessed foods, and the juices they produce. These living foods meet and satisfy the nutritional needs of our living cells. Living foods prevent uncontrollable hunger, produce abundant energy, and create vibrant health. Your daily intake of these foods should account for 85% of your total diet, or more.		
Beverages	Freshly extracted vegetable juices; BarleyMax, CarrotJuiceMax, BeetMax, distilled water.	
Dairy Alternatives	Fresh milk derived from oats, rice, coconut, nuts such as almond and hazelnut. Also, "fruit creams" made from strawberry, banana, blueberry.	
Fruits	All fresh, as well as organic, "unsulphered" dried fruit.	NOTE: Limit fruit to no more than 15% of daily raw food intake.
Grains	Soaked oats, millet, raw muesli, dehydrated granola or crackers, raw ground flaxseed, sprouted grains of all kinds.	
Beans	Green beans, peas, sprouted garbanzo beans, sprouted lentils, sprouted mung.	
Nuts and Seeds	Raw almonds, sunflower seeds, macadamia nuts, walnuts, raw almond butter, tahini.	NOTE: Consume nuts and seeds sparingly.
Oils and Fats	Extra virgin olive oil, grapeseed oil for cooking, Udo's Choice Perfected Oil Blend, flaxseed oil, avocados.	NOTE: Flax seed oil, particularly in the form of ground flax seeds, is the oil of choice for people with cancer.
Seasonings	Fresh and dehydrated herbs, garlic, sweet onions, parsley, salt-free seasonings.	
Soups	Raw soups.	
Sweets	Fruit smoothies, raw fruit pies with date/nut crusts, date/nut squares.	
Vegetables	All raw vegetables.	

Table 17

CATEGORY C—HALLELUJAH DIET FOODS–COOKED FOODS TO INCLUDE		
Cooked Foods (Ratio: 15%)		
We have already learned about the effects of high temperatures on food. The difference between raw and cooked food is the difference between life and death. Heat alters protein and destroys up to 83% of nutrients. But used sparingly, as 15% or less of your daily food intake, properly prepared cooked food can be delicious and satisfying. Also, they can help to maintain body weight, for those who don't have it to lose. Servings of these cooked foods should come after the raw food portions of your evening meal.		
Beverages	Caffeine-free herb teas, cereal-based coffee beverages, bottled organic juices.	
Beans	Lima, adzuki, black, kidney, navy, pinto, red, white, and other dried beans.	
Dairy Alternatives	Non-dairy cheese and milk, almond milk, nut butters.	NOTE: Use these items sparingly.
Fruit	Stewed/frozen unsweetened fruits.	
Grains	Whole grain cereals, breads, muffins, pasta, brown rice, spelt, amaranth, millet, etc.	
Oils	Mayonnaise made from cold-pressed oils, grapeseed oil for cooking.	
Seasonings	Light gray unrefined sea salt, cayenne pepper, all fresh or dried herbs.	NOTE: Use sparingly.
Soups	Soups made from scratch, without fat, dairy, table salt.	
Sweeteners	Raw, unfiltered honey, rice syrup, unsulphered molasses, stevia, carob, pure maple syrup, date sugar.	NOTE: Use these items sparingly.
Vegetables	Steamed or wok-cooked fresh or frozen vegetables, baked white or sweet potatoes, squash, etc.	

Table 18

Remember the amazing testimonies of those who put their faith in God rather than the crazy roller coaster of fast foods and pharmaceuticals? By doing so, they chose life over death and deadly illnesses. You've also learned what it takes to eliminate sickness from your own life and how your body contains the miraculous power to heal itself. And, from the charts on the previous pages, you have a basic knowledge of the living foods that make up 85 percent or more of the Hallelujah Diet. You also know the kinds of healthy cooked foods that should make up no more than 15 percent of your diet. Finally, you know the deadly foods you should avoid at all cost.

THE HALLELUJAH DIET BASIC DAILY PLAN

Now that you understand the "why" of *The Hallelujah Diet*, it's time to discover the "how" of it. But first, let's take a quick look at the basic daily plan of *The Hallelujah Diet*.

The Basic Hallelujah Diet		
Upon rising, take one serving of BarleyMax in powder form; dissolve it in your mouth or mix with a few ounces of distilled, room temperature water.		
BREAKFAST	NOTE: No cooked foods or foods containing fiber at this meal, as they hinder the cleansing process while the body eliminates accumulated toxins.	Note: BarleyMax is available in capsule who prefer it. NOTE: Children require a more substantial breakfast.
MID-MORNING SNACK	An 8-ounce glass of vegetable juice. NOTE: If not available, have a serving of CarrotJuiceMax or a piece of juicy, fresh fruit.	About 30 minutes later is an ideal time to use Fiber Cleanse as directed, B, Flax, D, or freshly ground flax seed.
Before lunch, have another serving of BarleyMax. Thirty minutes later, eat either a raw vegetable salad or raw fruit.		
LUNCH	NOTE: This should also be an uncooked meal. Fruit should be limited to no more than 15% of total daily intake.	Recommended for lunch: Recipe ideas: Raw Apple, Pear & Pecan Salad, Sprout Slaw, Dilly Zucchini, Greek Salad, Hallelujah Acres Blended Salad, Fantastic Salad, Better Than Tuna, or Fruit Smoothies.

MID-AFTERNOON SNACK	8-ounce glass of vegetable juice. NOTE: If not available, have a serving of CarrotJuiceMax, or some carrots or celery sticks.	Recipe ideas: fruit, Hummus, Apple Cinnamon Oatmeal Cookies, Snack Mix/Trail Mix, Carob Bars, Almond Butter Balls.
Before dinner, have another serving of BarleyMax. Thirty minutes later, eat a *large* green salad of leaf lettuce and a variety of vegetables. Then, eat a baked potato, brown rice, steamed veggies, whole grain pasta, or a veggie sandwich on whole grain bread.		
DINNER	NOTE: Do not eat head lettuce, as it has very little nutritional value. Remember to eat cooked foods *once* a day and limit to 15% of diet. Lunch and dinner meal can be switched.	Recipe ideas: Spicy Marinated Mixed Greens, Spinach Salad, Spaghetti, Lentils & Rice with Cucumber Salad, Ratatouille, Pasta with Broccoli and Pine Nuts, Portobello Philly Cheese Steak, Pecan Nut Loaf, Judy's Red Beans & Rice, Squash Supreme, or Chili.
If desired, eat a piece of juicy, fresh fruit or a glass of organic apple juice.		
EVENING SNACK		Recipe ideas: Banana Ice Cream, Blueberry Delight, Yummy Carob Pudding, or Corbin's Banana Mango Parfait.
For the recipes mentioned in this grid, go to the Recipe Index on page 361.		

Table 19

JOURNAL For WEEK 4—List A		
SAD Foods		
Look at the list on the right. Try to approximate as honestly as possible the **servings and quantities** of the **SAD foods** you consume regularly. Below, write down the foods from the SAD list that you eat in an average week.	Beverages	Alcohol, coffee, tea, cocoa, carbonated beverages and soft drinks, all artificial fruit drinks (including sports drinks), all commercial juices containing preservatives, refined salt, sweeteners.
Weekly Journal	Dairy	All animal-based milk, cheese, eggs, ice cream, whipped toppings, non-dairy creamers.
	Fruits	Canned and sweetened fruits, as well as non-organic dried fruits.
	Grains	Refined, bleached-flour products, cold breakfast cereals, white rice.
	Meats	Beef, pork, fish, chicken, turkey, hamburgers, hot dogs, bacon, sausage, etc.
	Nuts/Seeds	All roasted and/or salted seeds, nuts.
	Oils	All lard, margarine, shortenings; anything containing hydrogenated oils.
	Seasonings	Refined table salt, black pepper, any seasonings containing them.
	Soups	All canned or packaged soups, creamed soups that contain dairy products.
	Sweets	All refined white or brown sugar, sugar syrups, chocolate, candy, gum, cookies, donuts, cakes, pies, other products containing refined sugars or artificial sweeteners.
	Vegetables	All canned vegetables with added preservatives or vegetables fried in oil.

Table 20

JOURNAL FOR WEEK 4—LIST B		
LIVING FOODS		
Look at the list on the right. Try to approximate the **servings and quantities** of **living foods** you consume regularly. Below, write down the foods from the Living Foods list that you eat in one week.	Beverages	Freshly extracted vegetable juices (2/3 carrot and 1/3 greens), BarleyMax, CarrotJuiceMax, BeetMax, distilled water.
WEEKLY JOURNAL	Dairy Alternatives	Fresh milk derived from oats, rice, coconut, nuts such as almond and hazelnut. Also, "fruit creams" made from strawberry, banana, blueberry.
	Fruits	All fresh, as well as organic "unsulphered" dried fruit.
	Grains	Soaked oats, millet, raw muesli, dehydrated granola or crackers, raw ground flaxseed.
	Beans	Green beans, peas, sprouted garbanzo beans, sprouted lentils, sprouted mung.
	Nuts/Seeds	Raw almonds, sunflower seeds, macadamia nuts, walnuts, raw almond butter, tahini.
	Oils and Fats	Extra virgin olive oil, grapeseed oil for cooking, Udo's Choice Perfected Oil Blend, flaxseed oil, avocados.
	Seasonings	Fresh and dehydrated herbs, garlic, sweet onions, parsley, salt-free seasonings.
	Soups	Raw soups.
	Sweets	Fruit smoothies, raw fruit pies with date/nut crusts, date/nut squares.
	Vegetables	All raw vegetables.

Table 21

JOURNAL For WEEK 4—List C		
HALLELUJAH COOKED FOODS		
Look at the list on the right. Try to approximate the **servings and quantities** of healthy **cooked foods** you consume regularly. Below, write down the foods from the Cooked Foods list that you eat in one week.	Beverages	Caffeine-free herb teas, cereal-based coffee beverages, bottled organic juices.
WEEKLY JOURNAL	Dairy Alternatives	Non-dairy cheese and milk, almond milk, nut butters.
	Fruits	Stewed/frozen unsweetened fruits.
	Grains	Whole grain cereals, breads, muffins, pasta, brown rice, spelt, amaranth, millet, etc.
	Beans	Lima, adzuki, black, kidney, navy, pinto, red, white, and other dried beans.
	Oils and Fats	Mayonnaise made from cold-pressed oils, grapeseed oil for cooking.
	Seasonings	Light gray unrefined sea salt, cayenne pepper, all fresh or dried herbs.
	Soups	Soups made from scratch, without fat, dairy, table salt.
	Sweeteners	Raw, unfiltered honey, rice syrup, unsulphered molasses, stevia, carob, pure maple syrup, date sugar.
WEEKLY READING: *HOW DO I FEEL?*	Vegetables	Steamed/wok-cooked fresh or frozen vegetables, baked white or sweet potatoes, squash, etc.

Table 22

WEEK 5

I beseech you therefore, brethren, by the mercies of God, that ye present your bodies a living sacrifice, holy, [and] acceptable unto God. —Romans 12:1

WEEK 5 ASSIGNMENT

A. Read from *The Hallelujah Diet*:
   Chapter Four: The Real Miracle—Page 79
   Chapter Five: The Ways of Man and Medicine—Page 85
   Hallelujah Success Stories: Digestive Disorders—Page 165
   (Read first half, ending after "Rowen Pfeiffer")

B. Follow Part One—Study Guide, addressing all questions and activities.

C. Continue with Part Two—Journal for Week 5
   Read Chapter Twenty-two: Taking The First Steps—Page 269
   Continue with the Journal.

Part One—Study Guide

Fact-Finder Questions

1. We ought to take as much care of our physical health as we do of our spiritual well-being because _____ _____.

(Answer on page 81.)

2. According to Dr. Neal Barnard, "The real remedy to most digestive problems is so very basic, yet is hidden by the loud and deceptive barrage of advertising." The remedy he is referring to is:

    A) Tum-ta-Tum-Tums.
    B) Roto-rooter, that's the name.
    C) Asking your doctor if Prevacid is right for you.
    D) A healthy plant-based diet filled with natural fiber.

(Answer on page 166.)

3. Complete this sentence: "I wonder why we expect healing miracles when _____ _____."

(Answer on page 82.)

4. How many people die each year from iatrogenic causes? _____.

(Answer on page 85.)

5. How many people die each year from negative effects of pharmaceuticals? _____.
(Answer on page 85.)

6. Dr. Rowen Pfeiffer took his doctor's recommendation of Prednisone faithfully for one year to treat his ulcerative colitis. During that one year, along with "a whole laundry list of nasty side effects," the drug effectively turned off his _____ _____.

(Answer on page 168.)

7. The medical community is taught three basic modalities of treating disease. What are they?

A) _____

B) _____

C) _____

(Answer on page 86.)

8. On average, which of the following categories of people are the healthiest:

A) Doctors

B) Preachers

C) Nutritionists

D) Politicians

E) None of the above; they are equally unhealthy.

(Answer on page 89.)

Points to Ponder

1. Do you know anyone, including yourself, whose earthly mission may be cut short because of poor health? How do you think that situation could be prevented?

2. Do you think God—as the intelligent designer of the universe, and loving Father—would have allowed humanity to develop food supplies that make themselves sick? Is it possible we have led ourselves astray—away from our naturally health—promoting food supply—tempted by those who manipulate our health for financial gain?

3. Sometimes God requires us to take a "step of faith," such as when the Israelites began moving toward the Red Sea, or when a person first asks the Lord to enter his or her heart. This week, you will be advised to make a small step of faith by stopping the consumption of meat and dairy products. This may be a big jump for some of you. In two more weeks, however, once you have felt the effects of your initial "step of faith," you will be reading and understanding the reasons why you are feeling so much better. Are you willing to try changing your dietary direction for awhile?

Prayer & Reflection

Take a few moments to pray and reflect upon what you are studying. Here are a few prayer suggestions you may wish to add to your own:

Ask God to help you see how He connects the dots in the "big picture of life," with His plan to provide a health-promoting food supply—and many other natural gifts—to all living things.

Pray for insight about what the various foods you consume are doing to your health, either positively or negatively.

Seek wisdom about knowing when the responsibility for your health is in your own hands, and when that responsibility should be handed over to someone else.

Continue to pray for those who are sick, and when appropriate, pray for those individuals to receive insight into whether they have any choices in changing their own condition.

Highlights from Reading

We must abide by the natural law of Genesis 1:29 regarding proper fuel for nourishment of the physical body. By following God's natural law, we can learn how to eliminate sickness in our bodies and our lives.

My friends, if you are a follower of Jesus Christ, then God bought you lock, stock, and barrel—body, soul, and spirit—when you accepted Him as your Lord and Savior. And yet many people feel it's enough to serve Him *spiritually*, while still serving the world *physically*. They remain guided by their own childish appetites and take their nutritional wisdom from whatever Madison Avenue and commercial culture feeds them. What they don't realize is that if they don't take care of this temple (their body), the Holy Spirit will not have a place to indwell in this world. We ought to take as much care of our physical health as of our spiritual well-being because it all belongs to God.

We are so willing to go to a medical doctor, who will put poisonous toxic drugs into our bodies; or we submit to radiation or surgery in an effort to affect a cure. We spend a fortune and search the world to find cures for our physical problems, and yet we forget that inside each of us is a miraculous, built-in, self-healing mechanism called an *immune system*.

If the medical community could get the results we are getting here at Hallelujah Acres, it would be front-page headlines in tomorrow's newspaper and on TV evening news programs across the country. But I can almost guarantee you the solution to the physical ills of this world will never come from the top down, because there is too much money and too much politics in sickness.

Here's the fork in the road: if there is no designer, then it follows that there is no design, or connection, between separate parts of creation. In that scenario, anything goes and we should randomly try curing symptoms as they appear. But if there *is* an intelligent designer, then shouldn't we be looking to Him for clues about how it all fits together? The food designed to grow on this planet is a part of the same system God designed to nourish and build the cells inside our bodies. Modern medicine simply doesn't connect the dots between the cause and effect relationship between nutrition and health."People pay an enormous amount of money for laxatives to deal with constipation. But if we could get people on a healthy plant-based diet that gets the natural fiber into their diet, these laxative industries would probably be in liquidation in about a week," Dr. Neal Barnard says with a smile.

Tips &
Quotable Quotes

Calumet baking powder does not contain aluminum, which has been linked to promoting Alzheimer's disease.

"Leave your drugs in the chemist's pot if you can heal the patient with food." Hippocrates, the Father of Medicine

"There is no question that the people of this nation should be educated to consume more of the natural foods—and to stop the use of so many unworthy substitutes. Today folks are realizing that the best medicine is food." Royal S. Copeland, U. S. Senator (New York)

PART TWO — JOURNAL

Be sure you've read Chapter Twenty-two, Taking The First Steps, before continuing.

You've already been using the charts for several weeks to Journal your intake of SAD foods, living foods, and Hallelujah cooked foods. We hope that you are now sufficiently aware of the foods that pass through your lips, and have become motivated to begin replacing SAD foods with healthy alternatives.

Today we will focus on another tool, the Replacement Transition Journal, designed to help you reach your destination of replacing the bad old habits with good new ones. Of course, those who are facing an immediate health crisis should not be following the Maintenance (or transition) schedule, but should be taking the rapid Recovery track as discussed in Week 3. But for those who are not on the Recovery program, the aim is to set a realistic timetable for you to make the transition to the Hallelujah Diet, and for you to set your own pace in doing so. We suggest that every week you replace *at least* one bad old habit (food type from List A) with one good new habit (food type from Lists B and C). You are certainly encouraged to transition more rapidly if you wish, and if you do so you will see quicker results. But the important thing is to *always be moving in the right direction*.

Suggestion: To help in the transition process, try replacing entire meals with recipes found in the Recipe section of *The Hallelujah Diet* book. This will help you understand how the replacement foods actually fit into practical use. You might start by replacing main dishes or just side dishes. The important thing is to move in a positive direction, taking permanent steps toward better health.

After you have finished the Replacement Transition Journal exercise, continue your Journal entries for this week.

REPLACEMENT TRANSITION JOURNAL

Replace *Dairy*: All animal-based milk, cheese, eggs, ice cream, whipped toppings, nondairy creamers.

With *Dairy Alternatives*: Fresh milk from oats, rice coconut, nuts such as almond and hazelnut. And, "fruit creams" made from strawberry, banana, or other fruits.

WEEKLY REPLACEMENT JOURNAL

You are beginning Week 5 and are scheduling transitions through Week 12 of the Workbook. However, if you wish to transition even more slowly, beyond the end of the Workbook, you can continue on the blank pages provided and set your own pace.

WEEK 5 ____ / ____ / ____

REPLACE:

WITH:

WEEK 6 ____ / ____ / ____

REPLACE:

WITH:

WEEK 7 ____ / ____ / ____

REPLACE:

WITH:

WEEK 8 ____ / ____ / ____

REPLACE:

WITH:

WEEK 9 ____ / ____ / ____

REPLACE:

WITH:

WEEK 10 ____ / ____ / ____

REPLACE:

WITH:

WEEK 11 ____ / ____ / ____

REPLACE:

WITH:

WEEK 12 ____ / ____ / ____

REPLACE:

WITH:

WEEKLY JOURNAL CONTINUED
WEEK ____ / ____ / ____
REPLACE:
WITH:
WEEK ____ / ____ / ____
REPLACE:
WITH:
WEEK ____ / ____ / ____
REPLACE:
WITH:
WEEK ____ / ____ / ____
REPLACE:
WITH:
WEEK ____ / ____ / ____
REPLACE:
WITH:
WEEK ____ / ____ / ____
REPLACE:
WITH:
WEEK ____ / ____ / ____
REPLACE:
WITH:
WEEK ____ / ____ / ____
REPLACE:
WITH:
WEEK ____ / ____ / ____
REPLACE:
WITH:
WEEK ____ / ____ / ____
REPLACE:
WITH:

Table 23

JOURNAL FOR WEEK 5—LIST A		
SAD FOODS		
Look at the list on the right. Try to approximate as honestly as possible the **servings and quantities** of the **SAD foods** you consume regularly. Below, write down the foods from the SAD list that you eat in an average week.	Beverages	Alcohol, coffee, tea, cocoa, carbonated beverages and soft drinks, all artificial fruit drinks (including sports drinks), all commercial juices containing preservatives, refined salt, sweeteners.
WEEKLY JOURNAL	Dairy	All animal-based milk, cheese, eggs, ice cream, whipped toppings, non-dairy creamers.
	Fruits	Canned and sweetened fruits, as well as non-organic dried fruits.
	Grains	Refined, bleached-flour products, cold breakfast cereals, white rice.
	Meats	Beef, pork, fish, chicken, turkey, hamburgers, hot dogs, bacon, sausage, etc.
	Nuts/Seeds	All roasted and/or salted seeds, nuts.
	Oils	All lard, margarine, shortenings; anything containing hydrogenated oils.
	Seasonings	Refined table salt, black pepper, any seasonings containing them.
	Soups	All canned or packaged soups, creamed soups that contain dairy products.
	Sweets	All refined white or brown sugar, sugar syrups, chocolate, candy, gum, cookies, donuts, cakes, pies, other products containing refined sugars or artificial sweeteners.
	Vegetables	All canned vegetables with added preservatives or vegetables fried in oil.

Table 24

JOURNAL FOR WEEK 5—LIST B		
LIVING FOODS		
Look at the list on the right. Try to approximate the **servings and quantities** of **living foods** you consume regularly. Below, write down the foods from the Living Foods list that you eat in one week.	Beverages	Freshly extracted vegetable juices (2/3 carrot and 1/3 greens), BarleyMax, CarrotJuiceMax, BeetMax, distilled water.
WEEKLY JOURNAL	Dairy Alternatives	Fresh milk derived from oats, rice, coconut, nuts such as almond and hazelnut. Also, "fruit creams" made from strawberry, banana, blueberry.
	Fruits	All fresh, as well as organic "unsulphered" dried fruit.
	Grains	Soaked oats, millet, raw muesli, dehydrated granola or crackers, raw ground flaxseed.
	Beans	Green beans, peas, sprouted garbanzo beans, sprouted lentils, sprouted mung.
	Nuts/Seeds	Raw almonds, sunflower seeds, macadamia nuts, walnuts, raw almond butter, tahini.
	Oils and Fats	Extra virgin olive oil, grapeseed oil for cooking, Udo's Choice Perfected Oil Blend, flaxseed oil, avocados.
	Seasonings	Fresh and dehydrated herbs, garlic, sweet onions, parsley, salt-free seasonings.
	Soups	Raw soups.
	Sweets	Fruit smoothies, raw fruit pies with date/nut crusts, date/nut squares.
	Vegetables	All raw vegetables.

Table 25

JOURNAL FOR WEEK 5—LIST C		
HALLELUJAH COOKED FOODS		
Look at the list on the right. Try to approximate the **servings and quantities** of healthy **cooked foods** you consume regularly. Below, write down the foods from the Cooked Foods list that you eat in one week.	Beverages	Caffeine-free herb teas, cereal-based coffee beverages, bottled organic juices.
WEEKLY JOURNAL	Dairy Alternatives	Non-dairy cheese and milk, almond milk, nut butters.
	Fruits	Stewed/frozen unsweetened fruits.
	Grains	Whole grain cereals, breads, muffins, pasta, brown rice, spelt, amaranth, millet, etc.
	Beans	Lima, adzuki, black, kidney, navy, pinto, red, white, and other dried beans.
	Oils and Fats	Mayonnaise made from cold-pressed oils, grapeseed oil for cooking.
	Seasonings	Light gray unrefined sea salt, cayenne pepper, all fresh or dried herbs.
	Soups	Soups made from scratch, without fat, dairy, table salt.
	Sweeteners	Raw, unfiltered honey, rice syrup, unsulphered molasses, stevia, carob, pure maple syrup, date sugar.
WEEKLY READING: *How Do I Feel?*	Vegetables	Steamed/wok-cooked fresh or frozen vegetables, baked white or sweet potatoes, squash, etc.

Table 26

WEEK 6

The patient should be made to understand that he or she must take charge of his own life. Don't take your body to the doctor as if he were a repair shop. —Quentin Regestein, researcher, Harvard Medical School

Sickness is the vengeance of nature for the violation of her laws. —Charles Simmons

WEEK 6 ASSIGNMENT

A. Read from *The Hallelujah Diet*:
Chapter Six: God's Way: Living Food—Page 91
Chapter Seven: Proper Fuel for Miracles—Page 107
Hallelujah Success Stories: Digestive Disorders—Page
165
(Read second half, starting with Bill, Page 171)

B. Follow Part One—Study Guide, addressing all questions
and activities.

C. Continue with Part Two—Journal for Week 6

Part One—Study Guide

Fact-Finder Questions

1. The simple yet brilliant way God designed to pass along His life-giving energy from one living thing to another is in the form of _____ _____.
(Answer on page 91.)

2. List the damage inflicted upon our food when we heat it.
    A) Enzymes are lost
    B) Proteins are denatured
    C) Heated oils and fats convert to trans-fatty acids, which are carcinogenic
    D) Sugars are caramelized
    E) Vitamins and minerals become less available
    F) Other _____
    G) All of the above
(Answer on page 92.)

3. A daily dose of empty cooked foods—often in excess—leaves our body handicapped when it attempts to rebuild our cells or perform other important metabolic functions. What are some of the difficulties our bodies may encounter after consuming these foods for many years? _____, _____, _____, _____, and _____.
(Answer on pages 92-93.)

4. Living foods still contain their life-force, indicated by the presence of _____. (circle one)
    A) carbon
    B) active enzymes
    C) regular breathing
    D) a 60-cycle hum
(Answer on page 93.)

5. At what temperature do the enzymes—the life-force in food—begin to break down? _____.
(Answer on page 93.)

6. What happened to the zoo animals in the 1920s when the zookeepers began feeding them cooked meat? They _____ _____. (Answer on page 94-95.)

7. At Hallelujah Acres, we believe there are two important things one must do to rid the body of physical problems. What are they?

A) _____
_____, and

B) _____
_____.

(Answer on page 108.)

8. List at least five traits of a carnivore.

A) _____
B) _____
C) _____
D) _____
E) _____

(Answer on page 111.)

9. True or False: Raw fruits are the greatest source of all minerals and the second greatest source of all vitamins. _____.
(Answer on page 96.)

Points to Ponder

1. The typical American diet of today has little resemblance to the natural way of eating enjoyed by our earliest ancestors, or by contemporary wildlife in the natural kingdom. Compare those natural diets to the foods you have eaten in the past 24 hours. Which of your selections today would you describe as *living foods*, and which would you describe as *dead foods*?

2. If humans share so many more physiological traits with herbivores than with carnivores, then why do you suppose we find ourselves in a world in which people eat what they were not designed to eat? Could it have to do with our ability to adapt to temporarily harsh living conditions? If so, why do you think some segments of American society have adopted carnivorous eating habits to such an extreme degree?

3. It is true that our tastes adjust to whatever they eat regularly, although our digestive system is unable to adapt to eating improper foods for the long haul. The good news is that our tastes can adapt to enjoy new foods and tastes, once we condition ourselves to eat more sensibly. What do you feel will be the biggest adjustments you have to make personally—changing from the Standard American Diet to a more healthy one—in both letting go of familiar foods, and acquiring new tastes?

Prayer & Reflection

Take a few moments to pray and reflect upon what you are studying. Here are a few prayer suggestions you may wish to add to your own:

Ask God to give you a clear understanding of the vast system He created, in which animals absorb their energy from *living food.*

Spend some time in nature this week, and look for at least three examples of the eating habits of wildlife. Notice if any of them destroyed the nutrition in their food before eating.

Reflect on the underlying reasons why humanity strayed away from that basic diet of *living foods* to which all other species on earth adhere. Pray for hope, strength, and determination as you make your best efforts to change some of your old eating habits this week.

Thank God for the miraculous self-healing qualities He built into your "glorious and wonderfully made" body.

Highlights from Reading

In addition to our typically poor choices of foods, we compound the problem by cooking them. Think about putting your hand into boiling water for a few moments. Pretty destructive, don't you think? Now imagine food that is baked, broiled, or barbecued!

Living foods still contain their life-force, which is indicated by the presence of active enzymes. Those enzymes supplied in all living foods are crucial to proper digestion and absorption of the nutrients found in that food.

When we cook or process food at 107 degrees or higher, we modify the nutrients and reduce or, in some cases, completely eliminate their value. The body then has to work harder to move the dead, unnatural substance through the digestive system, causing great stress on the colon and robbing other organs of their enzymes. When we cook our food, we lose up to 97 percent of some water-soluble vitamins like Vitamin C and up to 40 percent of the lipid soluble vitamins.

A diet of *living foods* is not something that's just for old people; it's not just for sick people. This is the way God designed the human body to function! A living organism is designed to be fueled with energized, living foods and not devitalized, dead, cooked foods.

In the beginning, our brilliant Designer installed into our ancestors a genetic code for a triage—a portable M.A.S.H. unit—complete with painkillers for emergencies, antibiotics for infections, dressings for wounds, and microsurgery wards capable of replacing damaged cells with brand new ones. Each of us has *miraculous self-healing qualities* built into every nook and cranny of our body.

The next time you're in a crowded room—whether there are a hundred, a thousand, or ten thousand people—realize that if nobody changes what they eat, one of out three of them will die of a cardiovascular disease; one out of four will die of cancer; and the remaining people will die of complications from other diseases that were mainly preventable.

Although doctors describe G.E.R.D. (Gastroesophageal Reflux Disease) as chronic diseases, I am convinced that a simple change of diet is all that's needed to correct the problem. Here at Hallelujah Acres, we have heard hundreds of stories from people whose heartburn and G.E.R.D. symptoms disappeared after adopting the Hallelujah Diet.

Tips &
Quotable Quotes

Fruit is the perfect convenience health food. Naturally packaged in single servings, it keeps well at room temperature and can satisfy your sweet tooth as a between-meals snack.

"A disease is to be cured naturally by man's own power—and physicians help it." Hippocrates

"The physician of tomorrow will be the nutritionist of today." Thomas A. Edison

PART TWO—JOURNAL

Continue your Journal entries for this week, and refer back to this week's replacement goal in the Replacement Transition Journal (from Week 5).

WEEKLY REPLACEMENT TRANSITION JOURNAL
WEEK 6 ____ / ____ / ____
REPLACE:
WITH:

JOURNAL FOR WEEK 6—LIST A		
SAD FOODS		
Look at the list on the right. Try to approximate as honestly as possible the **servings and quantities** of the **SAD foods** you consume regularly. Below, write down the foods from the SAD list that you eat in an average week.	Beverages	Alcohol, coffee, tea, cocoa, carbonated beverages and soft drinks, all artificial fruit drinks (including sports drinks), all commercial juices containing preservatives, refined salt, sweeteners.
WEEKLY JOURNAL	Dairy	All animal-based milk, cheese, eggs, ice cream, whipped toppings, non-dairy creamers.
	Fruits	Canned and sweetened fruits, as well as non-organic dried fruits.
	Grains	Refined, bleached-flour products, cold breakfast cereals, white rice.
	Meats	Beef, pork, fish, chicken, turkey, hamburgers, hot dogs, bacon, sausage, etc.
	Nuts/Seeds	All roasted and/or salted seeds, nuts.
	Oils	All lard, margarine, shortenings; anything containing hydrogenated oils.
	Seasonings	Refined table salt, black pepper, any seasonings containing them.
	Soups	All canned or packaged soups, creamed soups that contain dairy products.
	Sweets	All refined white or brown sugar, sugar syrups, chocolate, candy, gum, cookies, donuts, cakes, pies, other products containing refined sugars or artificial sweeteners.
	Vegetables	All canned vegetables with added preservatives or vegetables fried in oil.

Table 27

JOURNAL FOR WEEK 6—LIST B		
LIVING FOODS		
Look at the list on the right. Try to approximate the **servings and quantities** of **living foods** you consume regularly. Below, write down the foods from the Living Foods list that you eat in one week.	Beverages	Freshly extracted vegetable juices (2/3 carrot and 1/3 greens), BarleyMax, CarrotJuiceMax, BeetMax, distilled water.
WEEKLY JOURNAL	Dairy Alternatives	Fresh milk derived from oats, rice, coconut, nuts such as almond and hazelnut. Also, "fruit creams" made from strawberry, banana, blueberry.
	Fruits	All fresh, as well as organic "unsulphered" dried fruit.
	Grains	Soaked oats, millet, raw muesli, dehydrated granola or crackers, raw ground flaxseed.
	Beans	Green beans, peas, sprouted garbanzo beans, sprouted lentils, sprouted mung.
	Nuts/Seeds	Raw almonds, sunflower seeds, macadamia nuts, walnuts, raw almond butter, tahini.
	Oils and Fats	Extra virgin olive oil, grapeseed oil for cooking, Udo's Choice Perfected Oil Blend, flaxseed oil, avocados.
	Seasonings	Fresh and dehydrated herbs, garlic, sweet onions, parsley, salt-free seasonings.
	Soups	Raw soups.
	Sweets	Fruit smoothies, raw fruit pies with date/nut crusts, date/nut squares.
	Vegetables	All raw vegetables.

Table 28

JOURNAL FOR WEEK 6—LIST C		
HALLELUJAH COOKED FOODS		
Look at the list on the right. Try to approximate the **servings and quantities** of healthy **cooked foods** you consume regularly. Below, write down the foods from the Cooked Foods list that you eat in one week.	Beverages	Caffeine-free herb teas, cereal-based coffee beverages, bottled organic juices.
WEEKLY JOURNAL	Dairy Alternatives	Non-dairy cheese and milk, almond milk, nut butters.
	Fruits	Stewed/frozen unsweetened fruits.
	Grains	Whole grain cereals, breads, muffins, pasta, brown rice, spelt, amaranth, millet, etc.
	Beans	Lima, adzuki, black, kidney, navy, pinto, red, white, and other dried beans.
	Oils and Fats	Mayonnaise made from cold-pressed oils, grapeseed oil for cooking.
	Seasonings	Light gray unrefined sea salt, cayenne pepper, all fresh or dried herbs.
	Soups	Soups made from scratch, without fat, dairy, table salt.
	Sweeteners	Raw, unfiltered honey, rice syrup, unsulphered molasses, stevia, carob, pure maple syrup, date sugar.
WEEKLY READING: *How Do I Feel?*	Vegetables	Steamed/wok-cooked fresh or frozen vegetables, baked white or sweet potatoes, squash, etc.

Table 29

WEEK 7

One personal choice seems to influence long-term health prospects more than any other—what we eat! —C. Everett Koop, M.D., U.S. Surgeon General, 1981-1988

WEEK 7 ASSIGNMENT

A. Read from *The Hallelujah Diet*:
  Chapter Eight: Dead Animal Products—Page 113
  Hallelujah Success Stories: Cardiovascular Disease—
    Page 261
  Chapter Twenty-three: Warning Label: Prepare for
    Detox—Page 277

B. Follow Part One—Study Guide, addressing all questions
  and activities.

C. Continue with Part Two—Journal for Week 7

PART ONE—STUDY GUIDE

Fact-Finder Questions

1. Briefly describe four of the reasons you might want to avoid foods with a face.

        A) _____

        B) _____

        C) _____

        D) _____

(Answers on page 113.)

2. Circle any that apply. All raw fruits and vegetables contain:

        A) Insulin

        B) Protein

        C) Prozac

        D) Vitamins and minerals

(Answer on page 114.)

3. How much fat does the average person consume in one year? _____.

(Answer on page 115.)

4. Besides the pesticides, other contaminants like _____, _____, and _____ also find their way into the commercially produced milk.

(Answers on page 118.)

5. Dr. T. Colin Campbell's 40 years of research on diet and disease concludes that even small intakes of _____ _____ are associated with significant increase in chronic degenerative diseases.

(Answers on page 119.)

6. What percentage of American men and women die of cardiovascular disease each year? Circle one.

        A) 21 percent

        B) 7 percent

        C) 34 percent

        D) 96 percent

(Answer on page 261.)

7. TRUE or FALSE:
   A) Before 1900, cardiovascular disease was hardly known and extremely rare. T / F
   B) Cardiovascular disease began with the advent of hydrogenated oils (margarine) and the processing (refining) of our grain foods such as wheat, corn, rye, barley, oats, and others, in which all the vital fatty acids are removed from these grains. T / F
   C) Heart attack is the number one cause of on-the-job deaths of firemen because putting out fires is such scary work. T / F

(Answers on pages 262-263.)

8. As we change from the SAD, dead food diet to the Hallelujah Diet filled with clean, living, nutritious, and fibrous foods, several things start to take place in our bodies. We begin a detoxification process—a cleansing reaction sometime known as a *healing crisis*. What are some symptoms of a healing crisis?

_____

_____

_____

(Answer on page 277.)

Points to Ponder

1. If you wonder whether you are a natural carnivore or herbivore, consider the following. Given the choice, what would be more appetizing to you: raw, freshly killed mammals, fish, and fowl; or raw, freshly picked fruits, vegetables, and nuts? If you had been born and raised without tools or the refinements of civilization to serve up meat in a pre-slaughtered and packaged condition—dressed beyond any recognition of the animal it had been—and then cooked into a bloodless taste and consistency, would you be inclined to pounce on an animal, kill it with your teeth and claws, then eat it raw? Would you be willing to try it, to prove you are a natural carnivore?

2. The research of Dr. Colin Campbell has shown that in various populations of the world where people consume very little or no animal products, they experience a correspondingly low incidence of heart disease, cancer, diabetes, and other degenerative disease. Do you think that we prosperous, meat-eating Americans have come to believe that these diseases are a "normal" part of life, simply because we see them all around us? What do you think it would take for the average American to recognize the link between eating animal products and bad health, such as what happened 50 years ago with the linkage of cigarette smoking and lung cancer?

3. The process of detoxification is often uncomfortable, such as getting headaches when one quits drinking coffee. Sometimes detox tests one's resolve to remain committed and suffer through the withdrawal pains until the body has purified itself. Here's a question that might help you get through the discomfort of detox: if your best friend was trying to give up drinking alcohol, and you saw him suffering nightsweats, would you give him a drink of alcohol to get over the symptoms? Or if he was trying to quit smoking and you saw him pacing the floor, would you give him a cigarette to help him calm down? Think of your body as your best friend, and when it gets past the discomfort, it will thank you!

Prayer & Reflection

Take a few moments to pray and reflect upon what you are studying. Here are a few prayer suggestions you may wish to add to your own:

Ask the Lord to help you understand your own body, and to give you extra sensitivity to recognize responses to various things you eat and drink.

Pray for wisdom to sort out all the conflicting messages you may be getting—from your reading, from television commercials, or from your Aunt Martha—about what is good, and good for you to eat.

Thank God for giving you a body that will serve you faithfully as a vehicle for your soul, as long as you faithfully fill it with the right grade of fuel.

Ask for extra strength to face the trials your body may experience when going through the detoxification process.

Highlights from Reading

If there is protein in the flesh of an animal, then where did all that protein come from? It came directly from the grass it ate! If there's calcium in the cow's milk, where did all that calcium come from? The grass! All the nutrients in an animal first came through the raw vegetation it ate. And when you eat the animal, you are getting the nutrients secondhand.

If you eliminate animal products from your diet, you eliminate the risk of experiencing a heart attack by 90 percent. If you don't consume animal products and you don't smoke, you reduce your risk of cancer almost completely. If you don't consume animal products, you reduce the probability of adult onset diabetes to nearly zero.

Another injury from a meat-based diet is the acidifying effect on our body's pH balance. The high volume of protein from meats causes an excess of acidity in our bodies, which greatly reduces the alkalinity in our bodies. The most acidifying foods are animal products like meats, poultry, fish, dairy, and eggs. A heightened acidic content in bodily fluids is the ultimate environment for promoting disease and ill health.

If we keep throwing acid products into our mouths, the body has to find a way to neutralize that acidity. The most alkaline substance in the greatest quantity in our bodies is calcium; and so the body literally must go into the bone and teeth to extract enough calcium to neutralize the acidity caused by the consumption of animal products and other things like soda pop. As a result, we eventually develop osteoporosis.

I was told I had cancer because my mother had colon cancer—that it was genetic. But when I changed what I ate, the cancer went away. So was it in the genes? Or was it in the diet?

The problem, according to Dr. Rowen Pfeiffer, is that "we see people all around us—they're getting to be middle-aged, and we expect them to have a few chronic health problems, such as heart disease. We think *this must be normal*! But it's *not* normal; it's just very common. And common is not normal. Being sick is not normal. We're meant to be healthy into a ripe old age."

While observing other parts of the world, we find that heart disease is virtually nonexistent, primarily due to the fact that people of other cultures subsist on a plant-based diet. In places like rural China, the Papua Islands, and Central Africa, for instance, coronary artery disease is practically nonexistent.

Seventy-six percent of all firemen over the age of 55 die of heart disease. It's because of these biological weapons of mass destruction that are flooding the firehouses: doughnuts, cookies, crackers, lunch meats, hot dogs, greasy food, and fast food.

We are literally digging our graves with our knives and forks in this country. And we're spreading this dangerous American style of eating all over the world. In fact, if we wanted to scientifically design a diet to create an epidemic of heart disease, cancer, and obesity, we couldn't do a better job than utilizing the diet style that Americans are eating today.

Tips &
Quotable Quotes

> "A low-fat, plant-based diet would not only lower the heart attack rate about 85 percent, but would lower the

cancer rate 60 percent." William Castelli, M.D., Director, Framingham Health Study

"In regions where meat is scarce, cardiovascular disease is unknown." *Time* magazine

"A large and convincing body of evidence from studies in humans show that diets low in saturated fatty acids and cholesterol are associated with low risks of cardio-vascular disease." U.S. National Research Council

Part Two—Journal

Continue your Journal entries for this week, and refer back to this week's replacement goal in the Replacement Transition Journal (from Week 5).

Weekly Replacement Transition Journal
Week 7 ___ / ___ / ___
Replace: With:

JOURNAL FOR WEEK 7—LIST A		
SAD FOODS		
Look at the list on the right. Try to approximate as honestly as possible the **servings and quantities** of the **SAD foods** you consume regularly. Below, write down the foods from the SAD list that you eat in an average week.	Beverages	Alcohol, coffee, tea, cocoa, carbonated beverages and soft drinks, all artificial fruit drinks (including sports drinks), all commercial juices containing preservatives, refined salt, sweeteners.
WEEKLY JOURNAL	Dairy	All animal-based milk, cheese, eggs, ice cream, whipped toppings, non-dairy creamers.
	Fruits	Canned and sweetened fruits, as well as non-organic dried fruits.
	Grains	Refined, bleached-flour products, cold breakfast cereals, white rice.
	Meats	Beef, pork, fish, chicken, turkey, hamburgers, hot dogs, bacon, sausage, etc.
	Nuts/Seeds	All roasted and/or salted seeds, nuts.
	Oils	All lard, margarine, shortenings; anything containing hydrogenated oils.
	Seasonings	Refined table salt, black pepper, any seasonings containing them.
	Soups	All canned or packaged soups, creamed soups that contain dairy products.
	Sweets	All refined white or brown sugar, sugar syrups, chocolate, candy, gum, cookies, donuts, cakes, pies, other products containing refined sugars or artificial sweeteners.
	Vegetables	All canned vegetables with added preservatives or vegetables fried in oil.

Table 30

JOURNAL FOR WEEK 7—LIST B		
LIVING FOODS		
Look at the list on the right. Try to approximate the **servings and quantities** of **living foods** you consume regularly. Below, write down the foods from the Living Foods list that you eat in one week.	Beverages	Freshly extracted vegetable juices (2/3 carrot and 1/3 greens), BarleyMax, CarrotJuiceMax, BeetMax, distilled water.
WEEKLY JOURNAL	Dairy Alternatives	Fresh milk derived from oats, rice, coconut, nuts such as almond and hazelnut. Also, "fruit creams" made from strawberry, banana, blueberry.
	Fruits	All fresh, as well as organic "unsulphered" dried fruit.
	Grains	Soaked oats, millet, raw muesli, dehydrated granola or crackers, raw ground flaxseed.
	Beans	Green beans, peas, sprouted garbanzo beans, sprouted lentils, sprouted mung.
	Nuts/Seeds	Raw almonds, sunflower seeds, macadamia nuts, walnuts, raw almond butter, tahini.
	Oils and Fats	Extra virgin olive oil, grapeseed oil for cooking, Udo's Choice Perfected Oil Blend, flaxseed oil, avocados.
	Seasonings	Fresh and dehydrated herbs, garlic, sweet onions, parsley, salt-free seasonings.
	Soups	Raw soups.
	Sweets	Fruit smoothies, raw fruit pies with date/nut crusts, date/nut squares.
	Vegetables	All raw vegetables.

Table 31

JOURNAL FOR WEEK 7—LIST C		
HALLELUJAH COOKED FOODS		
Look at the list on the right. Try to approximate the **servings and quantities** of healthy **cooked foods** you consume regularly. Below, write down the foods from the Cooked Foods list that you eat in one week.	Beverages	Caffeine-free herb teas, cereal-based coffee beverages, bottled organic juices.
WEEKLY JOURNAL	Dairy Alternatives	Non-dairy cheese and milk, almond milk, nut butters.
	Fruits	Stewed/frozen unsweetened fruits.
	Grains	Whole grain cereals, breads, muffins, pasta, brown rice, spelt, amaranth, millet, etc.
	Beans	Lima, adzuki, black, kidney, navy, pinto, red, white, and other dried beans.
	Oils and Fats	Mayonnaise made from cold-pressed oils, grapeseed oil for cooking.
	Seasonings	Light gray unrefined sea salt, cayenne pepper, all fresh or dried herbs.
	Soups	Soups made from scratch, without fat, dairy, table salt.
	Sweeteners	Raw, unfiltered honey, rice syrup, unsulphered molasses, stevia, carob, pure maple syrup, date sugar.
WEEKLY READING: *HOW DO I FEEL?*	Vegetables	Steamed/wok-cooked fresh or frozen vegetables, baked white or sweet potatoes, squash, etc.

Table 32

WEEK 8

I count him braver who overcomes his desires than him who conquers his enemies; for the hardest victory is the victory over self. —Aristotle

It is not the great temptations that ruin us; it is the little ones. —John W. DeForest, American Civil War novelist (1826-1906)

Opportunity may knock only once, but temptation leans on the doorbell. —Unknown

It is not the mountains that we conquer, but ourselves. —Sir Edmund Hillary, first to ascend Mt. Everest, 1953

WEEK 8 ASSIGNMENT

A. Read from *The Hallelujah Diet*:
    Chapter Nine: Other Dead and Deadly Products—
    Page 121
    Hallelujah Success Stories: Autoimmune Disorders—
    Page 237

B. Follow Part One—Study Guide, addressing all questions and activities.

C. Continue with Part Two—Journal for Week 8

Part One—Study Guide

Fact-Finder Questions

1. Why do food companies take healthful fruits and vegetables and embalm them with chemical preservatives, flavor-enhancers, and other compounds?
   A) To preserve enzymatic activity
   B) To enhance vitamin potency
   C) To glorify God's beautiful creations
   D) To extend shelf life
(Answer on page 121.)

2. Consuming just three sodas—or the equivalent of 33 teaspoons of sugar—will knock out your _____ _____ for how long? _____.
(Answer on page 123.)

3. TRUE or FALSE
   A) Ice cream is 37 percent sugar. T / F
   B) Many breakfast cereals are only 10 percent sugar. T / F
   C) Depression is one of the most rapidly growing problems in our society today. T / F
   D) Ritalin, used to treat ADHD, is also used as a street drug in Europe. T / F
(Answers on pages 123-124.)

4. *Circle the correct answer(s).* A low sodium diet will reduce the risk of:
   A) Hypertension and its complications.
   B) Kidney stones and stomach cancer.
   C) Complications of congestive heart failure.
   D) Cirrhosis of the liver, and osteoporosis.
   E) All of the above.
(Answers on page 125.)

5. Name four foreign invaders that your body's immune system is designed to protect against.
   A) _____
   B) _____

Prison Book Project
P.O. Box 1146
Sharpes, FL 32959

111

C) _____

D) _____

(Answers on page 237.)

   6. TRUE or FALSE:
      A) Problems with the immune system can only be contracted by contact with someone with HIV or AIDS. T / F
      B) Lupus is always fatal, and cannot be cured. T / F
      C) An autoimmune disorder diagnosis can prevent a person from obtaining car insurance. T / F

(Answers on page 238.)

   7. Which is more harmful to the body?
      A) Sugar sweetened soda
      B) Artificially sweetened soda

(Answer on page 128.)

   8. One of the greatest uses of refined, bleached, enriched white flour is that it can be used to make a wonderful _____.
(Answer on page 127.)

   9. Caffeine's _____ causes leeching of calcium from bone mass, which contributes greatly to osteoporosis.
(Answer on page 128.)

Points to Ponder

   1. Most pet owners would never dream of filling their pet's bowl with soda instead of water; or fill their food bowl with potato chips instead of pet food. And yet it has become socially acceptable to give this type of food and drink to our own human children. Youngsters become hooked on these addictive substances, preferring them to real and nutritious foods. Whose responsibility do you think it should be to correct this problem? The FDA? The food manufacturers? The surgeon general? The school system? The parents and children themselves?

2. A body is like a bank account of life-sustaining chemical compounds, which accumulates most effectively in our early "formative years." However, if we make only withdrawals and insufficient deposits throughout our adult years, we will find ourselves bankrupt of vital minerals, enzymes, and other compounds necessary for sustaining life, and our health becomes, predictably, "poor." When you look at the overall nutritional value in your grocery cart this week, think about the value of your deposits. Will they be enough to keep a "positive bank balance" in your body's account? Name at least five (or more) items that went into your cart this week that provided absolutely no positive nutritional value, ranking among the "dead and deadly foods."

3. The body's immune system is an incredibly powerful network of defenses to protect you from foreign invaders, like a well-organized homeland security system. But imagine what disasters would happen on a national level if we supplied our U.S. Army and National Guard with liquor instead of helicopter fuel, or cases of cookies instead of first-aid kits! It would be equally shortsighted to expect your body's immune system to do its job if you always send it junk food instead of the proper ammunition and provisions it needs to fight your battles. Now, put yourself in the place of a heroic antibody in some remote corner of your sickened body, facing a terrible enemy but without proper reinforcements! Quickly draft a short message to the commander back at headquarters, explaining your specific situation:

Prayer & Reflection

Take a few moments to pray and reflect upon what you are studying. Here are a few prayer suggestions you may wish to add to your own:

Reflect this week on the profound difference between food that contains active "life" and food that is "dead" or devitalized of anything that can support life in your body.

Ask God for wisdom about what you can do to help boost your own immune system by sending necessary provisions to your cells.

Find words to express thanks and gratitude for the amazingly well-designed system of health that God created within your body.

Pray for strength to face any old habits, perhaps acquired in childhood, and to exert the necessary willpower to get over the "hump" of breaking those addictions.

Take a deep breath, and consider the following statement: "I am not strong enough to overcome my weaknesses by myself but I can do whatever I decide to do, through the love of Christ who strengthens me."

Highlights from Reading

The next time you go to a supermarket to gather your family's food supply, think about this: after you've passed through the colorful displays of fruits and fresh vegetables in the produce department and you begin the long trek through aisle after aisle of boxes, cans, packages, jars, and various other containers of processed foods, you will have literally left the living food section of the store and entered the dead foods section. Lester Roloff—the man who first enlightened me to the life-giving miracle of raw foods—called these aisles of the supermarket mausoleums. He said, "That's where the dead food lies in state."

This may come as quite a shock to some of you, but all canned, jarred, and even most frozen products have already been heated—that's right; they've already been cooked! The living enzymes had to be destroyed because, if left intact, the food would have a very short shelf life.

Toxic food additives are put into our food supply for the sole purpose of fattening the bottom line of the parent company—with no consideration to the waistline or health of people who will consume the food.

Our wonderful, free enterprise economy has a built-in way of changing what companies sell us; it's called supply and demand. If we demand better quality, companies will figure out how to supply it to us. I assure you, a little time spent reading labels will reward you with a shopping cart that is virtually free of chemical additives.

Here in America, we just don't get enough omega-3 fatty acids, leafy greens, and natural foods in the amounts we need for normalcy. Instead, we eat a diet rich in refined foods, like white flour and sugar. Then we pour oil on it. The body is so deficient. Why would we expect the immune system to develop normally?

Dr. Joel Furman says this about immune disorders: "Most of the diseases that afflict Americans, such as multiple sclerosis, asthma, rheumatoid arthritis, lupus, allergies, and eczema, literally don't occur in other cultures that have a high intake of raw plant food. Fortunately, we've seen tremendous progress, even reversal, of these diseases when people adopt a program of nutritional excellence."

"For a long time, fat has been blamed for heart disease and certain cancers," says Dr. Neal Barnard. "Well, it's not so hot for your immune system either! If you take a blood sample and look at it under a powerful microscope, you see all the red blood cells that carry oxygen. But you also see white blood cells. Those are the soldiers in your immune system. They can swallow viruses, swallow cancer cells, and digest them. That's the way your immune system works. But they can't work in an oil slick. If you have a lot of grease in your diet interfering with the function of these blood cells, their ability to recognize invaders and to engulf them is diminished."

"We just have to intercede and teach people a way they can protect themselves," says Dr. Fuhrman, "literally show them how to arm their bodies with the ability to fight illness. And to do this, they just need to achieve normalcy—just have normal nutrition, which is eating real food, not fake food."

"When the body is gummed up with sugar, white flour products, and chemicals, the immune system turns on itself," adds Dr. Pfeiffer. "It's confused—it's not a healthy immune system. But when you get the body detoxified and cleaned out, it works the way it was designed."

Tips &
Quotable Quotes

> Used in moderation, raw maple syrup and raw honey are easily digestible replacements for sugar.

> Whole spelt flour is a great substitute for wheat flour, with a light and fluffy texture for baking.

> Thirty minutes of aerobic activity in the morning can give you a bigger energy boost than two cups of coffee.

> "The beef industry has contributed to more deaths than all the wars of this century, all natural disasters, and all automobile accidents combined. If beef is your idea of 'real food for real people,' you'd better live real close to a real good hospital." Neal Barnard, M.D., President's Committee for Responsible Medicine

PART TWO—JOURNAL

Continue your Journal entries for this week, and refer back to this week's replacement goal in the Replacement Transition Journal (from Week 5).

WEEKLY REPLACEMENT TRANSITION JOURNAL
WEEK 8 ___ / ___ / ___
REPLACE:
WITH:

JOURNAL FOR WEEK 8—LIST A		
SAD FOODS		
Look at the list on the right. Try to approximate as honestly as possible the **servings and quantities** of the **SAD foods** you consume regularly. Below, write down the foods from the SAD list that you eat in an average week.	Beverages	Alcohol, coffee, tea, cocoa, carbonated beverages and soft drinks, all artificial fruit drinks (including sports drinks), all commercial juices containing preservatives, refined salt, sweeteners.
WEEKLY JOURNAL	Dairy	All animal-based milk, cheese, eggs, ice cream, whipped toppings, non-dairy creamers.
	Fruits	Canned and sweetened fruits, as well as non-organic dried fruits.
	Grains	Refined, bleached-flour products, cold breakfast cereals, white rice.
	Meats	Beef, pork, fish, chicken, turkey, hamburgers, hot dogs, bacon, sausage, etc.
	Nuts/Seeds	All roasted and/or salted seeds, nuts.
	Oils	All lard, margarine, shortenings; anything containing hydrogenated oils.
	Seasonings	Refined table salt, black pepper, any seasonings containing them.
	Soups	All canned or packaged soups, creamed soups that contain dairy products.
	Sweets	All refined white or brown sugar, sugar syrups, chocolate, candy, gum, cookies, donuts, cakes, pies, other products containing refined sugars or artificial sweeteners.
	Vegetables	All canned vegetables with added preservatives or vegetables fried in oil.

Table 33

JOURNAL FOR WEEK 8—LIST B		
LIVING FOODS		
Look at the list on the right. Try to approximate the **servings and quantities** of **living foods** you consume regularly. Below, write down the foods from the Living Foods list that you eat in one week.	Beverages	Freshly extracted vegetable juices (2/3 carrot and 1/3 greens), BarleyMax, CarrotJuiceMax, BeetMax, distilled water.
WEEKLY JOURNAL	Dairy Alternatives	Fresh milk derived from oats, rice, coconut, nuts such as almond and hazelnut. Also, "fruit creams" made from strawberry, banana, blueberry.
	Fruits	All fresh, as well as organic "unsulphered" dried fruit.
	Grains	Soaked oats, millet, raw muesli, dehydrated granola or crackers, raw ground flaxseed.
	Beans	Green beans, peas, sprouted garbanzo beans, sprouted lentils, sprouted mung.
	Nuts/Seeds	Raw almonds, sunflower seeds, macadamia nuts, walnuts, raw almond butter, tahini.
	Oils and Fats	Extra virgin olive oil, grapeseed oil for cooking, Udo's Choice Perfected Oil Blend, flaxseed oil, avocados.
	Seasonings	Fresh and dehydrated herbs, garlic, sweet onions, parsley, salt-free seasonings.
	Soups	Raw soups.
	Sweets	Fruit smoothies, raw fruit pies with date/nut crusts, date/nut squares.
	Vegetables	All raw vegetables.

Table 34

JOURNAL For WEEK 8—List C		
HALLELUJAH COOKED FOODS		
Look at the list on the right. Try to approximate the **servings and quantities** of healthy **cooked foods** you consume regularly. Below, write down the foods from the Cooked Foods list that you eat in one week.	Beverages	Caffeine-free herb teas, cereal-based coffee beverages, bottled organic juices.
WEEKLY JOURNAL	Dairy Alternatives	Non-dairy cheese and milk, almond milk, nut butters.
	Fruits	Stewed/frozen unsweetened fruits.
	Grains	Whole grain cereals, breads, muffins, pasta, brown rice, spelt, amaranth, millet, etc.
	Beans	Lima, adzuki, black, kidney, navy, pinto, red, white, and other dried beans.
	Oils and Fats	Mayonnaise made from cold-pressed oils, grapeseed oil for cooking.
	Seasonings	Light gray unrefined sea salt, cayenne pepper, all fresh or dried herbs.
	Soups	Soups made from scratch, without fat, dairy, table salt.
	Sweeteners	Raw, unfiltered honey, rice syrup, unsulphered molasses, stevia, carob, pure maple syrup, date sugar.
WEEKLY READING: *How Do I Feel?*	Vegetables	Steamed/wok-cooked fresh or frozen vegetables, baked white or sweet potatoes, squash, etc.

Table 35

WEEK 9

The best remedy for those who are afraid, lonely or unhappy is to go outside, somewhere where they can be quiet, alone with the heavens, nature and God. Because only then does one feel that all is as it should be and that God wishes to see people happy, amidst the simple beauty of nature. —Anne Frank (1929-1945)

The sun, with all those planets revolving around it and dependent upon it, can still ripen a bunch of grapes as if it had nothing else in the universe to do. —Galileo

The greatest wealth is health. —Virgil

WEEK 9 ASSIGNMENT

A. Read from *The Hallelujah Diet*:
   Chapter Eleven: Living and Organic Foods—Page 147
   Chapter Twelve: Juicing—Page 161
   Hallelujah Success Stories: Depression and Emotional
      Healing—Page 221
   (Read pages 221-224, stopping at Sandy's Story)

B. Follow Part One—Study Guide, addressing all questions
   and activities.

C. Continue with Part Two—Journal for Week 9

Part One—Study Guide

Fact-Finder Questions

1. What are the main differences between the 1996 USDA Food Pyramid and the most recent one? _____

_____

_____ .

(Answer on pages 148 & 150.)

2. What is included in the category of "Dead and Deadly Foods"? _____.

    A) Food that has had most of its enzymes and nutrients destroyed by cooking or processing.

    B) Foods that contain refined flour or refined sugar, which may actually draw stored vitamins from your body as your system tries to metabolize them.

    C) Foods that contain animal products.

    D) Caffeine.

    E) Refined salt.

    F) All the above.

(Answer on pages 150-151.)

3. List some of the health consequences of eating dead food.

_____

_____

_____

_____

_____

_____

_____

_____

_____

_____

_____

_____

_____

_____

(Answer on page 151.)

4. TRUE or FALSE:
   A) A healthy body is mostly acidic balanced. T / F (Answer on page 154.)
   B) When dead foods are consumed, diseases start forming; the colon becomes clogged; the cells become deprived of oxygen and other nutrients; and the blood's pH balance, which should be 7.35 to 7.4, moves down more toward the acidic range. T / F (Answer on page 154.)
   C) Foods like meat, cheese, white flour products, caffeine, and alcohol give the body a healthy edge over disease. T / F (Answer on page 151.)
   D) Eating living foods has a naturally alkalizing effect, thereby reversing the effects of an acidic diet. T / F

(Answer on page 154.)

5. The lower levels of nutrition in our modern food supply means we will have to consume more food to receive adequate nutrition. What is one effective way of accomplishing this?

_____.

(Answer on page 161.)

6. According to Dr. Neal Barnard, what are three common food substances we put into our mouths that can profoundly affect the way our brain functions and may lead to depression, phobias, compulsions, panic attacks, and other emotional problems?

   A) _____
   B) _____
   C) _____
(Answers on page 221.)

7. Emotional depression is one of the most rapidly growing problems in our society today. What is the primary way our society deals with it? _____
(Answer on page 222.)

Points to Ponder

1. The USDA-approved food pyramid—which many of us were raised believing to be the gospel truth in nutrition

information—turns out to be a collection of biased propaganda from an assortment of industrial lobbies. It promoted a ratio of foods that made the most economic sense to the manufacturers and growers of those foods. It even nodded to the totally useless sweets and hydrogenated fats as if eating them were a basic need (thank goodness it made no reference to tobacco or alcohol!). The strangest omission was any comment about eating *raw* fruits and vegetables, even though scientists of the day fully acknowledged the destruction of essential vitamins by cooking. Can you remember any credible sources of information in your life that spoke about eating living foods? When was the first time you ever had anyone bring to your attention the benefits of living foods?

2. The life force God puts into all living things is part of the life cycle, designed to be consumed for the continuation of that life force in another creature, like a flame passed along from one candle to another. What happens when the flame is blown out before reaching the next candle? What do you think happens to the cycle of life—as it relates to our body—when we extinguish the life force by cooking? And after years of consuming only food without its life force, what do you think would happen to your own life force?

3. Consider the amazing nutrient density of carrot juice. An organically grown California carrot grows deeply into rich, naturally composted soil and draws into itself a wide spectrum of trace minerals—creating one of the most potent organic foods

imaginable. Then 10 or 12 of these fresh, living carrots are juiced and consumed immediately, allowing that pure life force to be absorbed almost instantly, with little or no digestive effort to slow the process. Now picture your own cells receiving that life force and nutrition—perhaps more than it has received in years. Imagine the gratitude felt by each cell of your body. Spend a moment considering the love of God, as He passes along *life*, from one *life* form to another. Say or write down any thoughts that come to mind.

Prayer & Reflection

Take a few moments to pray and reflect upon what you are studying. Here are a few prayer suggestions you may wish to add to your own:

This is a good time to express gratitude for the *life* that God put into your body, and into all living creatures.

Reflect on the meaning and mystery of the transitory energy we call *life*.

Pray for wisdom regarding the relationship we have with other life forms, at the miraculous intersection in which our own life force is fed by that of another.

Next mealtime, consider the loving relationship one can have with that *life* that is given to sustain yours, by giving thanks before eating.

Love, joy, peace, patience, and many other emotions are called the fruits of the Spirit. Reflect for a few minutes on the beautiful imagery of healthy fruits passing along the *life force* from a healthy vine, and enjoyed in good health by others in creation.

Highlights from Reading

Juices made from fresh vegetables are also living foods. The nutrients in fresh juices are full of vitamins, minerals, amino acids, and enzymes. The best advantage of drinking fresh vegetable juice rather than eating the whole vegetable is that the fiber has been removed, and thus we get more nutrition to the cellular level of our bodies much more quickly. Less energy is expended in assimilating it because our bodies aren't trying to separate the juice from the fiber (which is not absorbed by the body but expelled as waste).

The bottom line is that living foods bring us life. A diet rich in living foods as designed by God and with everything we need for perfect health provides us with the ultimate raw materials to not only *maintain optimal health and vigor*, but also to *heal ourselves* of existing disease and sickness.

The vibrant flavors alone are enough reason for many people to prefer organic produce, and the assurance of a food supply free of toxic pesticides and chemicals makes it a wise choice, especially for those battling sickness. It takes the stress off your body. And since it tastes better, you'll want to eat more of it, thereby increasing the quality of your health.

One of the best values in organic produce is California carrots, which can be purchased in bulk and are the very best to use for juicing and salads. The flavor is outstanding and will encourage you to drink and eat these nutrient-dense organic gems in large, healthy quantities.

Something most people don't realize is that there's no nutrition in fiber! If fiber could enter the blood stream, it would clog up our whole system. The nutrients are in the liquid parts of the fruits and vegetables we eat—not in the fibrous parts.

Give your experience with juicing plenty of time, and try bringing an optimistic attitude into it. Make it like an expedition into new territory with the hope of discovering something new and amazing! Hundreds of thousands of people have now experienced juicing and follow the Hallelujah Diet. We are all here to encourage you to step out and take responsibility for your health with God's help. He has given you all the wisdom and resources you need to enjoy the many benefits of living His way.

"When a person gets on a very healthy, plant-based diet, they quite often report two things," Dr. Neal Barnard says. "Their energy level improves; instead of sleeping eleven hours a day, they're getting just a normal night's sleep and they have more energy as the day goes by; they're feeling good about the world they live in."

Dr. Shawn Pallotti says, "Many people today are just worn out and they don't know why. They're taking various medications, eating a poor diet, and then wondering why they don't feel happy. I think it's really just another way of the body saying, *something is wrong.* A dehydrated, highly medicated, caffeine- and sugar-stimulated body cannot have joy; it cannot have peace of mind and clarity."

Tips &
Quotable Quotes

> Dehydrating your own apples, bananas, tomatoes, eggplant and many other fruits and vegetables (at a temperature below 107 degrees) can be a fun family activity, and can provide you with living foods that can be stored without refrigeration.

> You can make wonderful living food treats in a food processor by combining things like dates, raisins, raw almonds, raw pumpkin seeds, raw sesame seeds, unhulled sesame seeds, and similar foods—even adding CarrotMax, BarleyMax, and BeetMax—to invent your own super food confections.

> Deep breathing can help calm stressed nerves. If you feel anxiety or depression creeping up, put on an exercise video or do other stretching and breathing exercises to send oxygen to your brain and body.

"No pharmacist will ever compound a pill, patent a medicine or drug that can compare in curative value with the value found in uncooked, pure fruit and vegetable juices." H.E. Kirschner, M.D., *Live Food Juices*

PART TWO—JOURNAL

Continue your Journal entries for this week, and refer back to this week's replacement goal in the Replacement Transition Journal (from Week 5).

WEEKLY REPLACEMENT TRANSITION JOURNAL
WEEK 9 ____ / ____ / ____
REPLACE:
WITH:

JOURNAL For WEEK 9—List A		
SAD Foods		
Look at the list on the right. Try to approximate as honestly as possible the **servings and quantities** of the **SAD foods** you consume regularly. Below, write down the foods from the SAD list that you eat in an average week.	Beverages	Alcohol, coffee, tea, cocoa, carbonated beverages and soft drinks, all artificial fruit drinks (including sports drinks), all commercial juices containing preservatives, refined salt, sweeteners.
WEEKLY JOURNAL	Dairy	All animal-based milk, cheese, eggs, ice cream, whipped toppings, non-dairy creamers.
	Fruits	Canned and sweetened fruits, as well as non-organic dried fruits.
	Grains	Refined, bleached-flour products, cold breakfast cereals, white rice.
	Meats	Beef, pork, fish, chicken, turkey, hamburgers, hot dogs, bacon, sausage, etc.
	Nuts/Seeds	All roasted and/or salted seeds, nuts.
	Oils	All lard, margarine, shortenings; anything containing hydrogenated oils.
	Seasonings	Refined table salt, black pepper, any seasonings containing them.
	Soups	All canned or packaged soups, creamed soups that contain dairy products.
	Sweets	All refined white or brown sugar, sugar syrups, chocolate, candy, gum, cookies, donuts, cakes, pies, other products containing refined sugars or artificial sweeteners.
	Vegetables	All canned vegetables with added preservatives or vegetables fried in oil.

Table 36

JOURNAL FOR WEEK 9—LIST B		
LIVING FOODS		
Look at the list on the right. Try to approximate the **servings and quantities** of **living foods** you consume regularly. Below, write down the foods from the Living Foods list that you eat in one week.	Beverages	Freshly extracted vegetable juices (2/3 carrot and 1/3 greens), BarleyMax, CarrotJuiceMax, BeetMax, distilled water.
WEEKLY JOURNAL	Dairy Alternatives	Fresh milk derived from oats, rice, coconut, nuts such as almond and hazelnut. Also, "fruit creams" made from strawberry, banana, blueberry.
	Fruits	All fresh, as well as organic "unsulphered" dried fruit.
	Grains	Soaked oats, millet, raw muesli, dehydrated granola or crackers, raw ground flaxseed.
	Beans	Green beans, peas, sprouted garbanzo beans, sprouted lentils, sprouted mung.
	Nuts/Seeds	Raw almonds, sunflower seeds, macadamia nuts, walnuts, raw almond butter, tahini.
	Oils and Fats	Extra virgin olive oil, grapeseed oil for cooking, Udo's Choice Perfected Oil Blend, flaxseed oil, avocados.
	Seasonings	Fresh and dehydrated herbs, garlic, sweet onions, parsley, salt-free seasonings.
	Soups	Raw soups.
	Sweets	Fruit smoothies, raw fruit pies with date/nut crusts, date/nut squares.
	Vegetables	All raw vegetables.

Table 37

JOURNAL FOR WEEK 9—LIST C		
HALLELUJAH COOKED FOODS		
Look at the list on the right. Try to approximate the **servings and quantities** of healthy **cooked foods** you consume regularly. Below, write down the foods from the Cooked Foods list that you eat in one week.	Beverages	Caffeine-free herb teas, cereal-based coffee beverages, bottled organic juices.
WEEKLY JOURNAL	Dairy Alternatives	Non-dairy cheese and milk, almond milk, nut butters.
	Fruits	Stewed/frozen unsweetened fruits.
	Grains	Whole grain cereals, breads, muffins, pasta, brown rice, spelt, amaranth, millet, etc.
	Beans	Lima, adzuki, black, kidney, navy, pinto, red, white, and other dried beans.
	Oils and Fats	Mayonnaise made from cold-pressed oils, grapeseed oil for cooking.
	Seasonings	Light gray unrefined sea salt, cayenne pepper, all fresh or dried herbs.
	Soups	Soups made from scratch, without fat, dairy, table salt.
	Sweeteners	Raw, unfiltered honey, rice syrup, unsulphered molasses, stevia, carob, pure maple syrup, date sugar.
WEEKLY READING: *How Do I Feel?*	Vegetables	Steamed/wok-cooked fresh or frozen vegetables, baked white or sweet potatoes, squash, etc.

Table 38

WEEK 10

For fast-acting relief, try slowing down. —Lily Tomlin

Half our life is spent trying to find something to do with the time we have rushed through life trying to save. —Will Rogers, Autobiography, 1949

Sometimes the most important thing in a whole day is the rest we take between two deep breaths. —Etty Hillesum, Jewish diarist (1914-1943)

WEEK 10 ASSIGNMENT

A. Read from *The Hallelujah Diet*:
    Chapter Seventeen: Exercise—Page 209
    Chapter Eighteen: Stress and Emotional Balance—
    Page 213
    Chapter Nineteen: Rest—Page 233
    Hallelujah Success Stories: Depression and Emotional
    Healing—Page 221
    (Read the second half on Stress)

B. Follow Part One—Study Guide, addressing all questions
    and activities.

C. Continue with Part Two—Journal for Week 10

PART ONE—STUDY GUIDE

Fact-Finder Questions

1. TRUE or FALSE:
   A) Without exercise, tissue cells retain more elasticity. T / F
   B) Without exercise, lymph nodes cannot release all their toxins because the lymphatic system doesn't have a pump like the heart; it uses the body's movements to help circulate its fluids. T / F
   C) Without exercise, muscles atrophy. T / F
   D) Without exercise, the heart is strengthened against heart disease and other cardiovascular problems. T / F
   E) Without exercise, bones can lose density from lack of rebuilding; osteoporosis is the result. T / F

(Answers on pages 209-210.)

2. Name three different types of exercise to improve blood and lymph circulation that you should incorporate into your exercise regimen. _____, _____ and _____.
(Answers on pages 210-211.)

3. What is the first organ affected by a bad diet, because of its vulnerability to its own molecular balance? _____ _____.
(Answer on page 215.)

4. Can a healthy diet, especially one rich in living enzymes and nutrients, make up for the overuse and unending stress to which we often subject ourselves?
         Yes_____ No _____
(Answer on page 226.)

5. Finish this sentence:
         Nothing tastes as good as_____!
(Answer on page 219.)

6. How can someone like me, who consumed a diet of living foods and exercised vigorously, fall victim to a stroke?

    A) It is a genetically determined inevitability.

    B) One's body can become weak by an overexposure to phytochemicals.

    C) The body's response to prolonged and unrelieved stress, no matter how perfect one's diet and exercise program, can translate emotional tension into physical illness.

    D) A vegan tends to consume too much saturated fat, leading to a build up of plaque on the arteries, which may eventually lead to stroke.

(Answer on pages 229-230.)

7. Stress is a very real threat to our physical and emotional health. It is perhaps one of the greatest challenges in mastering oneself, to balance that eternal tension between _____

_____.

(Answer on page 232.)

8. Your body uses sleep to recharge and recover. While you sleep, it _____:

    A) Eliminates waste products.

    B) Circulates hormones and nutrients.

    C) Produces the infection—fighting compounds we need in order to recover from injury and illness.

    D) All of the above.

(Answer on pages 233-234.)

Points to Ponder

1. In bygone days, people exerted their bodies sufficiently to use up the adrenaline generated in everyday life. Even when not actually running from danger, they got plenty of exercise just doing the daily chores. But nowadays we don't run from wolves, or even hoe the fields for survival—some just click the computer—mouse faster and more furiously to stay alive. If the resulting muscle tension and increased heart—rate are not physically expended, then the naturally occurring *fight or flight* chemicals build up in our bodies and causes tremendous stress. It must

either be "burned up" with exercise—no matter how pointless that exertion may seem—or it will catch up with us like the wolf we didn't outrun, threatening to kill us through hypertension, stroke, or other disease. Can you name any instances when you felt emotional pressures turning into physical stress in your body? What physical activities do you find most effective in dissipating your stress?

2. Eating and emotions are closely linked. Many times people eat because they experience emotional triggers such as loneliness, frustration, or depression. Many foods affect our emotions directly, like the excitement one gets from caffeine or sugar, or the relaxation one feels from alcohol. People can experience long-term problems when their eating habits and emotions become linked by cycles of addictive dependency. Can you identify any foods you crave as the result of emotional triggers? Can you name "comfort foods" that make you feel better immediately after eating them? Now, can you honestly judge whether those foods make you feel better because they are nutritious, or because they have become linked to an emotional balancing act?

Prayer & Reflection

Take a few moments to pray and reflect upon what you are studying. Here are a few prayer suggestions you may wish to add to your own:

If you struggle with the idea of exercise, ask God to help you find a regular routine that you will enjoy enough to stay with—like prayerful walks, meditative swimming, or something else that exercises body and soul together.

Reflect on the biblical idea of *rest*. (See Jeremiah 6:16; 2 Thessalonians 1:7; Psalm 16:9.)If you feel stressed, "burdened or heavy—laden," about anything, take up the Lord's promise to help carry those problems and to "give you rest." (See Matthew 11:28.)Ask for wisdom about finding the right balance in your body and soul, such as a proper time and place for physical tasks verses physical rest, and mental tasks verses mental rest.

Highlights from Reading

Exercise is vital for our bodies. We were created to work and labor for our food and other personal needs. We're weaker than our forefathers in our bodies, not just because of our diets but also because of our sedentary lifestyles. Today most of us have standard desk jobs. We get up in the morning, go to work, sit at our desks for hours, and then go home. We push carts around a grocery store, collecting packaged food and paying with the money we earn by sitting at our desks.

Exercise can improve your intake of oxygen, which provides a burst of energy and increases your stamina; it helps the body produce new cells; it encourages better circulation; and it prevents many diseases.

Obesity is a simple math problem—we take in more calories than we burn, and thus we gain weight. Once we burn more calories than we're taking in, we lose weight and regulate our metabolism. While you may lose fat, you may still weigh the same as you tone your muscles, and they increase in mass and density.

The way your clothes fit is a better indicator than a scale when measuring your weight loss.

An unhealthy body is the home of an unhealthy mind; but as you detoxify your system, you free your mind as well.

Read the testimonies of those who have suffered needlessly from emotional and mental diseases. They changed their diet to the one God intended, and they were healed. There was no magic pill; they simply put the jumper cables of live food on their brain and gave it a positive charge.

Dr. Shawn Pallotti says, "When it comes to stress, our nation is burning the candle at both ends. We need to take time out for ourselves, for our family, and for God. We really need to put our priorities into perspective and figure out what's important to us."

Dr. Pallotti knows the importance of balancing rest and diet with a busy profession. "My energy solely comes from a natural diet of lots of raw foods and lots of fresh juice, where my body doesn't require all my blood down there to digest pancakes, waffles, sausages, and beer. If I had to do that, there's no way I could last half a day."

Friends, allow me to put my stroke experience into perspective with the Hallelujah Diet and lifestyle: my doctors consider my rapid recovery next to miraculous. They have all assured me that if I had not been in such good condition from years of good eating and exercise, I would certainly not be here today.

Rest is the reward for a day's faithful service; you can take it with confidence that whatever didn't get done today, God will bless your efforts to complete it tomorrow.

Tips &
Quotable Quotes

> "One of the most important of the methylxanthines is the popular drug 'caffeine.' Undesirable effects from the stimulating properties of caffeine include: elevated heart rate, irregular heartbeat, increased blood pressure, frequent urination, increased gastric acid secretion (which contributes to indigestion, gastritis, and ulcers), nervousness, irritability, insomnia, loss of appetite,

nausea, and diarrhea. Obviously, discontinuing caffeine will relieve the problems caused by this drug." Dr. John McDougall, *The McDougall Plan*

"Why should any Christian be surprised to find that modern science and personal experience confirm that 'God's Original Diet' of raw fruits and vegetables (Genesis 1:29) is the ideal diet for mankind?" Dr. George Malkmus, author and founder of Hallelujah Acres

"Nothing will benefit human health and increase the chances for survival of life on earth as much as the evolution to a vegetarian diet." Albert Einstein

Part Two—Journal

Continue your Journal entries for this week, and refer back to this week's replacement goal in the Replacement Transition Journal (from Week 5).

Weekly Replacement Transition Journal
Week 10 ___ / ___ / ___
Replace:
With:

JOURNAL FOR WEEK 10—LIST A		
SAD FOODS		
Look at the list on the right. Try to approximate as honestly as possible the **servings and quantities** of the **SAD foods** you consume regularly. Below, write down the foods from the SAD list that you eat in an average week.	Beverages	Alcohol, coffee, tea, cocoa, carbonated beverages and soft drinks, all artificial fruit drinks (including sports drinks), all commercial juices containing preservatives, refined salt, sweeteners.
WEEKLY JOURNAL	Dairy	All animal-based milk, cheese, eggs, ice cream, whipped toppings, non-dairy creamers.
	Fruits	Canned and sweetened fruits, as well as non-organic dried fruits.
	Grains	Refined, bleached-flour products, cold breakfast cereals, white rice.
	Meats	Beef, pork, fish, chicken, turkey, hamburgers, hot dogs, bacon, sausage, etc.
	Nuts/Seeds	All roasted and/or salted seeds, nuts.
	Oils	All lard, margarine, shortenings; anything containing hydrogenated oils.
	Seasonings	Refined table salt, black pepper, any seasonings containing them.
	Soups	All canned or packaged soups, creamed soups that contain dairy products.
	Sweets	All refined white or brown sugar, sugar syrups, chocolate, candy, gum, cookies, donuts, cakes, pies, other products containing refined sugars or artificial sweeteners.
	Vegetables	All canned vegetables with added preservatives or vegetables fried in oil.

Table 39

JOURNAL FOR WEEK 10—LIST B		
LIVING FOODS		
Look at the list on the right. Try to approximate the **servings and quantities** of **living foods** you consume regularly. Below, write down the foods from the Living Foods list that you eat in one week.	Beverages	Freshly extracted vegetable juices (2/3 carrot and 1/3 greens), BarleyMax, CarrotJuiceMax, BeetMax, distilled water.
WEEKLY JOURNAL	Dairy Alternatives	Fresh milk derived from oats, rice, coconut, nuts such as almond and hazelnut. Also, "fruit creams" made from strawberry, banana, blueberry.
	Fruits	All fresh, as well as organic "unsulphered" dried fruit.
	Grains	Soaked oats, millet, raw muesli, dehydrated granola or crackers, raw ground flaxseed.
	Beans	Green beans, peas, sprouted garbanzo beans, sprouted lentils, sprouted mung.
	Nuts/Seeds	Raw almonds, sunflower seeds, macadamia nuts, walnuts, raw almond butter, tahini.
	Oils and Fats	Extra virgin olive oil, grapeseed oil for cooking, Udo's Choice Perfected Oil Blend, flaxseed oil, avocados.
	Seasonings	Fresh and dehydrated herbs, garlic, sweet onions, parsley, salt-free seasonings.
	Soups	Raw soups.
	Sweets	Fruit smoothies, raw fruit pies with date/nut crusts, date/nut squares.
	Vegetables	All raw vegetables.

Table 40

JOURNAL FOR WEEK 10—LIST C		
HALLELUJAH COOKED FOODS		
Look at the list on the right. Try to approximate the **servings and quantities** of healthy **cooked foods** you consume regularly. Below, write down the foods from the Cooked Foods list that you eat in one week.	Beverages	Caffeine-free herb teas, cereal-based coffee beverages, bottled organic juices.
WEEKLY JOURNAL	Dairy Alternatives	Non-dairy cheese and milk, almond milk, nut butters.
	Fruits	Stewed/frozen unsweetened fruits.
	Grains	Whole grain cereals, breads, muffins, pasta, brown rice, spelt, amaranth, millet, etc.
	Beans	Lima, adzuki, black, kidney, navy, pinto, red, white, and other dried beans.
	Oils and Fats	Mayonnaise made from cold-pressed oils, grapeseed oil for cooking.
	Seasonings	Light gray unrefined sea salt, cayenne pepper, all fresh or dried herbs.
	Soups	Soups made from scratch, without fat, dairy, table salt.
	Sweeteners	Raw, unfiltered honey, rice syrup, unsulphered molasses, stevia, carob, pure maple syrup, date sugar.
WEEKLY READING: *HOW DO I FEEL?*	Vegetables	Steamed/wok-cooked fresh or frozen vegetables, baked white or sweet potatoes, squash, etc.

Table 41

WEEK 11

The best six doctors anywhere, and no one can deny it;
are sunshine, water, rest, and air, exercise, and diet.
These six will gladly you attend, if only you are willing.
Your mind they'll ease, your will they'll mend, and charge
you not a shilling.
—Nursery rhyme quoted by Wayne Fields, *What the*
River Knows, 1990

WEEK 11 ASSIGNMENT

A. Read from *The Hallelujah Diet*:
   Chapter Thirteen: Cleansing the System—Page 177
   Chapter Fourteen: Clean Water—Page 183
   Chapter Fifteen: Clean Air—Page 187
   Chapter Sixteen: Sunlight—Page 205
   Hallelujah Success Stories: Weight Loss and
      Management—Page 191
   (Read pages 191-198.)

B. Follow Part One—Study Guide, addressing all questions and activities.

C. Continue with Part Two—Journal for Week 11

Part One—Study Guide

Fact-Finder Questions

1. If you are like most people, you've probably spent your life eating dead, processed, and chemically laden foods. Many of the toxins from those foods are stored in your body. But as you consume clean, living food you will, in effect, be giving your body permission to finally get rid of those toxins. Sometimes this is an uncomfortable process. What is this process sometimes called? _____.
(Answer on page 177.)

2. What are the five eliminative exit points through which toxins leave your body?

A) _____
B) _____
C) _____
D) _____
E) _____

(Answers on page 178.)

3. TRUE or FALSE:

A) Water is not required to transport nutrients throughout the body through the bloodstream. T / F
B) Water stabilizes and cools us, allowing us to maintain proper body temperature. T / F
C) Our body is composed of 30 percent water. T / F
D) Water helps keep the colon clean. Our large intestine is like a sewer system; keeping the body hydrated helps keep it clean and waste moving through it. T / F

(Answers on pages 183-184.)

4. Name two additives that make municipal tap water an undesirable source for clean drinking and cooking water? _____, and _____.
(Answer on page 184.)

5. Complete this sentence: Many mental illnesses are the result of _____ _____.

(Answer on page 188.)

6. What foods should we consume that are rich in oxygen? _____.

(Answer on page 189.)

7. What is the protective mechanism (pigment) that healthy skin produces when exposed to the sun? _____ _____.

(Answer on page 205.)

8. Complete the sentence: Our skin is one of the last organs to receive attention from the inside of the body. This means that when you eat, the nourishment goes to the most important organs first, and whatever is left goes to your skin. Most people who live on an improper diet are _____ _____.

(Answer on page 206.)

Points to Ponder

1. Cleansing your system from years of collected toxins can create feelings of sickness, as the poisons again pass through your body on their way out. Don't mistake this as real illness, but instead as a natural sign that you are on the path to getting well. Can you list symptoms that other addictive substances generate, when a person's body is experiencing "cold turkey" withdrawal?

2. Clean water, clean air, and natural sunlight are some of the elements our body needs in order to return to a naturally balanced condition. However, water tainted by additives (chlorine, fluoride, caffeine, sweeteners, artificial flavors, and others), air polluted by smoke and chemical gasses, and artificial lights or

sudden overexposure to sunlight—all add up to a barrage of *unnatural* assaults on the body. Among the good habits we need to adopt—besides good eating—is to deliberately expose ourselves to environments where we can soak up these natural elements. Can you list some activities you can do to help you and your family to get a good measure of clean water, clean air, and sunshine every week?

WATER:

CLEAN AIR:

SUNSHINE:

3. America has seen the number of overweight children double in the past 30 years; currently 15 to 30 percent of school-aged kids in various regions of the country are considered obese! This will condemn these children to a life of heart disease, diabetes, and other weight-related sicknesses that could have been avoided. Put yourself in the place of a grandparent who is concerned about your grandchild's poor eating habits. Can you write down a polite but effective way of reminding the parents that the future health of their children relies upon the eating habits they learn before age 12? (Or maybe you are in the parent's place, respectfully asking grandma or grandpa to stop indulging the grandkids with junk food.)

Prayer & Reflection

Take a few moments to pray and reflect upon what you are studying. Here are a few prayer suggestions you may wish to add to your own:

God loves to hear appreciation for His creation. Take time to give thanks for the natural gifts we have been given: pure water, fresh air, radiant sunshine, and anything else for which you are grateful.

Pray for inspiration about finding opportunities that will put you into natural environments, like hiking, trips to the beach, gardening, horseback riding, or outdoor sports.

Reflect on times in your life when you may have felt truly pure and clear-headed, either by juice fasting, exercising, meditating, or being in nature. Reconnect to those feelings, and pray for insights as to how to increase those experiences.

Whenever you are faced with the urge to indulge or binge upon foods that you know will not contribute to a healthy life, ask God to lead you away from that temptation. He will always hear and grant that prayer, if you are sincere.

Highlights from Reading

As you consume clean, living food you will, in effect, be giving your body permission to finally get rid of those toxins. Sometimes this is an uncomfortable process. As your body begins dealing with the damage caused by your former lifestyle, you may experience symptoms that for a short time could actually make you feel worse. But my friends, please don't give up! The good health and energy you have so long desired is right around the corner.

Eyes, ears, nose, and throat. Your body uses all of these organs to detoxify. Many symptoms we consider illness are really just our bodies expelling unwanted particles out of our system.

Distilled water is the most reliable source these days for clean drinking and cooking water. It is produced by boiling water and then condensing the steam in a cooling coil that drips the water into a collector.

Deep breathing and exercise wake up your brain better than a jolt of caffeine ever would—and it's a lot better for your body. With increased oxygen intake, your brain becomes more alert and your mental capacity increases.

Disease is thwarted in an oxygenated environment. Sickness can't manage a foothold in a body that is full of oxygen. It was proven decades ago that cancer cells couldn't multiply in an oxygen-rich environment.

The fact is that our bodies have a built-in protection from the dangerous parts of the sun's radiation. This protective mechanism—melanin—is a pigment that healthy skin produces when exposed to the sun.

The Hallelujah Diet has actually aided many people suffering from skin cancers. It is quite possible that diet is the problem, not just overexposure to the sun. Recent research from Baylor College shows that a diet high in cooked fats and chemicals and low in leafy greens greatly increases the chance of skin cancer. So fearing skin cancer is relevant when you don't have the proper diet. The sun may cause inflammation in the skin that leads to cancer; but it's a poor, lifeless diet that inhibits the body's ability to heal the inflammation and repair the skin.

Tips &
Quotable Quotes

> "When your calorie needs are met, your protein needs are met." Dr. Joel Fuhrman, *Eat to Live*

> "Our bodies have a tremendous capacity to heal themselves. The catch is that we must give the body a chance to do so." Joel Robbins, D.C., M.D.

> "In the same way that a house is only as good as the quality of its materials, the body is only as strong as the quality of the nutrients it receives." Francisco Contreras, M.D.

PART TWO—JOURNAL

A. *Potluck Assignment*: This is the week to begin making plans for the upcoming Hallelujah Potluck meal! (Some have called this a *Raw-Luck Supper*, though others feel the name doesn't do justice to the delicacies you'll find, so you decide what to call it!) Make arrangements for when and where to hold the meal, and then decide on who brings what, in terms of dishes. Also, be sure someone is responsible for providing plates, utensils, napkins, and such.

Depending on how many participants you have to bring foods, try to dole out a good variety of salads and slaws, main dishes, and ethnic cuisine, as well as a few desserts for fun. We highly recommend that you choose your recipes from those in *The Hallelujah Diet* book, although your own raw-food creations would be welcome too. Some good cooks might be inspired to provide more than one dish, to ensure the meal's success. It is always good if people bring *tried and true* favorites, since many of you have been with the Hallelujah Diet for several months now and have auditioned various recipes.

Write down a few dishes you would like to suggest for the Potluck meal:

_____

_____

_____

B. Continue your Journal entries for this week, and refer back to this week's replacement goal in the Replacement Transition Journal (from Week 5).

WEEKLY REPLACEMENT TRANSITION JOURNAL
WEEK 11 ____ / ____ / ____
REPLACE:
WITH:

JOURNAL FOR WEEK 11—LIST A		
SAD FOODS		
Look at the list on the right. Try to approximate as honestly as possible the **servings and quantities** of the **SAD foods** you consume regularly. Below, write down the foods from the SAD list that you eat in an average week.	Beverages	Alcohol, coffee, tea, cocoa, carbonated beverages and soft drinks, all artificial fruit drinks (including sports drinks), all commercial juices containing preservatives, refined salt, sweeteners.
WEEKLY JOURNAL	Dairy	All animal-based milk, cheese, eggs, ice cream, whipped toppings, non-dairy creamers.
	Fruits	Canned and sweetened fruits, as well as non-organic dried fruits.
	Grains	Refined, bleached-flour products, cold breakfast cereals, white rice.
	Meats	Beef, pork, fish, chicken, turkey, hamburgers, hot dogs, bacon, sausage, etc.
	Nuts/Seeds	All roasted and/or salted seeds, nuts.
	Oils	All lard, margarine, shortenings; anything containing hydrogenated oils.
	Seasonings	Refined table salt, black pepper, any seasonings containing them.
	Soups	All canned or packaged soups, creamed soups that contain dairy products.
	Sweets	All refined white or brown sugar, sugar syrups, chocolate, candy, gum, cookies, donuts, cakes, pies, other products containing refined sugars or artificial sweeteners.
	Vegetables	All canned vegetables with added preservatives or vegetables fried in oil.

Table 42

JOURNAL FOR WEEK 11—LIST B		
LIVING FOODS		
Look at the list on the right. Try to approximate the **servings and quantities** of **living foods** you consume regularly. Below, write down the foods from the Living Foods list that you eat in one week.	Beverages	Freshly extracted vegetable juices (2/3 carrot and 1/3 greens), BarleyMax, CarrotJuiceMax, BeetMax, distilled water.
WEEKLY JOURNAL	Dairy Alternatives	Fresh milk derived from oats, rice, coconut, nuts such as almond and hazelnut. Also, "fruit creams" made from strawberry, banana, blueberry.
	Fruits	All fresh, as well as organic "unsulphered" dried fruit.
	Grains	Soaked oats, millet, raw muesli, dehydrated granola or crackers, raw ground flaxseed.
	Beans	Green beans, peas, sprouted garbanzo beans, sprouted lentils, sprouted mung.
	Nuts/Seeds	Raw almonds, sunflower seeds, macadamia nuts, walnuts, raw almond butter, tahini.
	Oils and Fats	Extra virgin olive oil, grapeseed oil for cooking, Udo's Choice Perfected Oil Blend, flaxseed oil, avocados.
	Seasonings	Fresh and dehydrated herbs, garlic, sweet onions, parsley, salt-free seasonings.
	Soups	Raw soups.
	Sweets	Fruit smoothies, raw fruit pies with date/nut crusts, date/nut squares.
	Vegetables	All raw vegetables.

Table 43

JOURNAL FOR WEEK 11—LIST C		
HALLELUJAH COOKED FOODS		
Look at the list on the right. Try to approximate the **servings and quantities** of healthy **cooked foods** you consume regularly. Below, write down the foods from the Cooked Foods list that you eat in one week.	Beverages	Caffeine-free herb teas, cereal-based coffee beverages, bottled organic juices.
WEEKLY JOURNAL	Dairy Alternatives	Non-dairy cheese and milk, almond milk, nut butters.
	Fruits	Stewed/frozen unsweetened fruits.
	Grains	Whole grain cereals, breads, muffins, pasta, brown rice, spelt, amaranth, millet, etc.
	Beans	Lima, adzuki, black, kidney, navy, pinto, red, white, and other dried beans.
	Oils and Fats	Mayonnaise made from cold-pressed oils, grapeseed oil for cooking.
	Seasonings	Light gray unrefined sea salt, cayenne pepper, all fresh or dried herbs.
	Soups	Soups made from scratch, without fat, dairy, table salt.
	Sweeteners	Raw, unfiltered honey, rice syrup, unsulphered molasses, stevia, carob, pure maple syrup, date sugar.
WEEKLY READING: *HOW DO I FEEL?*	Vegetables	Steamed/wok-cooked fresh or frozen vegetables, baked white or sweet potatoes, squash, etc.

Table 44

WEEK 12

The doctor of the future will give no medicine but will interest his patients in the care of the human frame in diet and in the cause and prevention of disease. —Thomas A. Edison, American inventor (1847-1931)

Nothing will benefit human health and increase the chances for survival of life on earth as much as the evolution to a vegetarian diet. —Albert Einstein, theoretical physicist (1879-1955)

WEEK 12 ASSIGNMENT

A. Read from *The Hallelujah Diet*:
   Chapter Twenty-four: In Love with Food All Over
      Again—Page 283
   Plus Skim through Recipes—Pages 286-331
   Hallelujah Success Stories: Weight Loss and
      Management—Page 191
   (Read the second half, pages 198-204)

B. Follow Part One—Study Guide, addressing all questions
   and activities.

C. Continue with Part Two—Journal for Week 12
   Journal: The "After Picture"

PART ONE—STUDY GUIDE

Fact-Finder Questions

1. On the Standard American Diet (SAD) our taste buds become desensitized. How does this happen? _____ _____.
(Answer on page 283.)

2. Aside from the neural damage discussed in an earlier chapter, what is one of the unfortunate side effects of consuming flavor enhancers used to "liven up" the tastes of dead foods? _____.
(Answer on page 283.)

3. Most people are excited to learn that the 100 trillion cells comprising their physical bodies are constantly _____ _____.
(Answer on pages 283-284.)

4. Different types of cells take varying amounts of time to regenerate.
        A) How long does it take to replace the bone structure of your body? _____
        B) How long does it take to replace our taste buds? _____
(Answers on page 284.)

5. In order to lose weight, what does Dr. Joel Fuhrman propose we do? _____ _____
(Answer on page 192.)

6. According to Dr. Fuhrman, a toxic diet causes _____ _____. But when you consume healthy foods, you lose the desire to constantly put food in your stomach.
(Answer on page 197.)

7. Which of the following two concerns should an overweight person focus on first?
        A) The condition of being overweight.
        B) The task of becoming healthy.
(Answer on page 197.)

Points to Ponder

1. Retraining your tastes can be a little like the process of teaching little children to try foods for the first time (remember the three-bite rule?). Did you know all baby animals naturally reject new foods, until the parent repeatedly "insists" they eat it? It is nature's way of protecting little ones from consuming what they shouldn't. Similarly, we grown humans often have the same response to new tastes, until we make ourselves eat something repeatedly. Write down and silently rehearse a loving response to yourself, to recite whenever you try eating something that might not excite your palate the first few times you eat it.

2. Our appetite for food is a natural driving force to assure we consume sufficient nutrition for survival. But if one's diet is devoid of real nourishment because of either A) too much junk food; B) an absence of nutrient-dense produce; or C) by simply cooking the vitamins and enzymes to death—then our appetites will continue to send us hunger signals, no matter how many calories we consume. Many people who go on the Hallelujah Diet discover that by giving their body a generous and well-balanced supply of nutritious foods, their appetite is satisfied long before they eat an excess of calories. Can you see how America can be a nation of both obese and malnourished people, all at the same time? Have you ever experienced an insatiable appetite, binging on unhealthy foods? What kinds of foods do people claim they *just can't get enough of* to satisfy?

3. Now that you've begun to experience the health improvements that come with a healthy diet, your friends, coworkers, and others will begin to notice. Some may even ask what you're doing differently; and you may be excited to tell them. What are the reactions you've encountered when you've shared your new-found insights on healthy eating? Has there been some resistance? How have you handled it?

Prayer & Reflection

Take a few moments to pray and reflect upon what you are studying. Here are a few prayer suggestions you may wish to add to your own: Thank God for your beautiful and miraculously self-healing body, and your discovery of how it functions best by eating the amazing living foods He created to nourish it.

Reflect upon the many insights you have gained in the past three months, particularly concerning God's phenomenal design for your happiness and well-being. Pray for all those who are suffering needlessly from degenerative disease throughout the world. Ask God to open their eyes, so that people everywhere can come to a collective understanding about what can be done to ease suffering.

If you are experiencing difficulty in describing your newly found energy and healthy lifestyle to others who may not want to hear about it, don't worry. Pray for wisdom about how and when to share your discoveries with those you love. Remember, one can teach best by example.

Highlights from Reading

People take the Standard American Diet style, which is very low in nutrients in the first place, and then try to eat *less* food, getting even fewer nutrients. It never works, because they are chronically craving food, constantly fighting their body's desire for more nutrition. They struggle with their cravings; measuring their food, weighing portion sizes, counting calories, and calculating fat percentages. In the end they gain more weight than they originally started with.

If you were drinking ten cups of coffee a day and you stopped drinking coffee, you'd feel sick for about four or five days. That's called withdrawal, and it leads to temporary symptoms like headaches, weakness, and shakes. But those ill feelings are actually beneficial. Your body is repairing the damage from the things you were taking that weren't healthy for you. Healthy substances like parsley, broccoli, string beans, and mangoes don't cause any (withdrawal) problems when you stop taking them. Only unhealthy substances cause those withdrawal-type symptoms.

Dr. Neal Barnard says, "It's not too late for turning things in the other direction. If we take these unhealthy foods out of our diet and follow a dietary pattern that is based on vegetables, fruits, and healthier plant-based foods, the weight loss is permanent. With a healthy diet, you get the fuel into your body that belongs there. You trim down. You get the waistline that nature had in mind for you, and it stays that way."

Within churches in the Bible belt, fried-chicken fellowships and potbellied pastors are as much a part of the culture as stock car races and sentences that start with "Y'all." Churches traditionally have not worried much about waistlines. As Autumn Marshall, a nutritionist at church-affiliated Lipscomb University in Tennessee, explaines, most evangelical Christians don't drink, smoke, curse, or commit adultery. "So what do we do?" she asked. "We eat!" "While the Bible frequently condemns gluttony," Marshall said, "it just appears to be a more acceptable vice."

"You'll see a group of people who have obviously been to church," Ed Young said, "and you'll see them order all this fat-laden food and then they'll say, 'Let's pray together: *God, bless this food to the nourishment of our bodies.*'" Young adds, "The deal is they should have prayed before they ordered, *'God, help me order stuff that will glorify You!'*

Fortunately, it only takes a short time to get our taste buds back in shape. Once you change your diet from the mostly dead, cooked, and processed foods of the SAD to the predominantly living, whole foods of the Hallelujah Diet, you'll begin to notice a growing appreciation for natural flavors.

Most people are excited to learn that the 100 trillion cells comprising their physical bodies are constantly dying and replacing themselves at approximately 300 million cells per minute. In other words, our bodies are continuously rebuilding themselves, one cell at a time.

Tips &
Quotable Quotes

> "Some people think if you change your diet to what George teaches, you will be hungry all the time. What I found was that when I changed my diet and began exercising, the hunger went away. You have to realize, it's a lifestyle change. It's not a fad and it's not just a diet." Rhonda Malkmus, cofounder of Hallelujah Acres

> "In the over 30 years since I recovered from colon cancer, one of the most basic and important things I have learned is that there is a vast difference between God's ways and man's ways." Dr. George Malkmus

> "The secret of a live, clean body is live, clean food—fresh vegetables, juices, fruit, and nice green salads. I do not live completely without a cook stove, but because of its overuse, it has become the murderer of the human race." Pastor Lestor Roloff

PART TWO—JOURNAL: THE "AFTER PICTURE"

A.   The After Picture: It is finally time to complete the following chart for your records. When you have finished, flip back to the charts you filled out in Week 2 to see how far you've come!

> *SUGGESTION: At the Hallelujah Potluck meal, it is good to go around the room and share the results from your "After Picture" with the people who have been participating in this study with you. You may want to stay in touch with these people in the future, so we have provided a place in the back of this book to share one another's contact information.*

B.   Journal: Continue your entries for this week, including the Replacement Transition Journal. You can decide if you wish to continue with your journaling from here forward. By now, you have probably acquired the habits that will propel you into a healthy future. If, however, you wish to continue to keep track now or at a future time, you can always print downloadable PDF files found at www.hallelujahdietbook. com.

The "AFTER PICTURE"

Week 12: PROGRESS REPORT : PHYSICAL, EMOTIONAL & SPIRITUAL

ENERGY LEVEL: On a scale between 1-10, (1 is lowest energy and 10 is highest energy), how would you rate your average energy level these days?

_____

Congratulations! You have completed the 12-week Hallelujah Diet study guide program. You have undoubtedly learned many new ideas about diet and health. You have also made some substantial changes to your own dietary habits. Here is an opportunity for a self-evaluation, measuring the results you've experienced in the past three months. Consider this your "After Picture," which you can compare side-by-side with the "Before Picture" you completed in Week 2.

Describe below how you feel—physically, emotionally, and spiritually—after experiencing the Hallelujah Diet.

ENERGY LEVEL: On a scale between 1-10, (1 is lowest energy and 10 is highest energy), how would you rate your average energy level these days?

_____

Physical:

Emotional:

Spiritual:

Table 45

Continue your Journal entries for this week, and refer back to this week's replacement goal in the Replacement Transition Journal (from Week 5).

WEEKLY REPLACEMENT TRANSITION JOURNAL
WEEK 12 ____ / ____ / ____
REPLACE:
WITH:

JOURNAL FOR WEEK 12—LIST A		
SAD FOODS		
Look at the list on the right. Try to approximate as honestly as possible the **servings and quantities** of the **SAD foods** you consume regularly. Below, write down the foods from the SAD list that you eat in an average week.	Beverages	Alcohol, coffee, tea, cocoa, carbonated beverages and soft drinks, all artificial fruit drinks (including sports drinks), all commercial juices containing preservatives, refined salt, sweeteners.
WEEKLY JOURNAL	Dairy	All animal-based milk, cheese, eggs, ice cream, whipped toppings, non-dairy creamers.
	Fruits	Canned and sweetened fruits, as well as non-organic dried fruits.
	Grains	Refined, bleached-flour products, cold breakfast cereals, white rice.
	Meats	Beef, pork, fish, chicken, turkey, hamburgers, hot dogs, bacon, sausage, etc.
	Nuts/Seeds	All roasted and/or salted seeds, nuts.
	Oils	All lard, margarine, shortenings; anything containing hydrogenated oils.
	Seasonings	Refined table salt, black pepper, any seasonings containing them.
	Soups	All canned or packaged soups, creamed soups that contain dairy products.
	Sweets	All refined white or brown sugar, sugar syrups, chocolate, candy, gum, cookies, donuts, cakes, pies, other products containing refined sugars or artificial sweeteners.
	Vegetables	All canned vegetables with added preservatives or vegetables fried in oil.

Table 46

JOURNAL FOR WEEK 12—LIST B		
LIVING FOODS		
Look at the list on the right. Try to approximate the **servings and quantities** of **living foods** you consume regularly. Below, write down the foods from the Living Foods list that you eat in one week.	Beverages	Freshly extracted vegetable juices (2/3 carrot and 1/3 greens), BarleyMax, CarrotJuiceMax, BeetMax, distilled water.
WEEKLY JOURNAL	Dairy Alternatives	Fresh milk derived from oats, rice, coconut, nuts such as almond and hazelnut. Also, "fruit creams" made from strawberry, banana, blueberry.
	Fruits	All fresh, as well as organic "unsulphered" dried fruit.
	Grains	Soaked oats, millet, raw muesli, dehydrated granola or crackers, raw ground flaxseed.
	Beans	Green beans, peas, sprouted garbanzo beans, sprouted lentils, sprouted mung.
	Nuts/Seeds	Raw almonds, sunflower seeds, macadamia nuts, walnuts, raw almond butter, tahini.
	Oils and Fats	Extra virgin olive oil, grapeseed oil for cooking, Udo's Choice Perfected Oil Blend, flaxseed oil, avocados.
	Seasonings	Fresh and dehydrated herbs, garlic, sweet onions, parsley, salt-free seasonings.
	Soups	Raw soups.
	Sweets	Fruit smoothies, raw fruit pies with date/nut crusts, date/nut squares.
	Vegetables	All raw vegetables.

Table 47

JOURNAL FOR WEEK 12—LIST C		
HALLELUJAH COOKED FOODS		
Look at the list on the right. Try to approximate the **servings and quantities** of healthy **cooked foods** you consume regularly. Below, write down the foods from the Cooked Foods list that you eat in one week.	Beverages	Caffeine-free herb teas, cereal-based coffee beverages, bottled organic juices.
WEEKLY JOURNAL	Dairy Alternatives	Non-dairy cheese and milk, almond milk, nut butters.
	Fruits	Stewed/frozen unsweetened fruits.
	Grains	Whole grain cereals, breads, muffins, pasta, brown rice, spelt, amaranth, millet, etc.
	Beans	Lima, adzuki, black, kidney, navy, pinto, red, white, and other dried beans.
	Oils and Fats	Mayonnaise made from cold-pressed oils, grapeseed oil for cooking.
	Seasonings	Light gray unrefined sea salt, cayenne pepper, all fresh or dried herbs.
	Soups	Soups made from scratch, without fat, dairy, table salt.
	Sweeteners	Raw, unfiltered honey, rice syrup, unsulphered molasses, stevia, carob, pure maple syrup, date sugar.
WEEKLY READING: *How Do I Feel?*	Vegetables	Steamed/wok-cooked fresh or frozen vegetables, baked white or sweet potatoes, squash, etc.

Table 48

NOTES AND REMINDERS		

CONTACT INFORMATION FOR **HALLAULUJAH DIET STUDY GROUP:**		

Notes for Group Leaders

This will be an exciting 12 weeks for you and your group. It will provide many opportunities to explore profound questions about God's miraculous design for optimal health in these beautiful bodies He gave us. Thank you for taking responsibility for not only your own health-consciousness, but for helping other people to think carefully about this much-neglected yet crucial component of their earthly life. *May God bless you greatly!*

For those using this workbook in a group study, we suggest one person be appointed as group leader. The following section is written to you as the group leader, to give you a track to run on. It will provide a practical outline for how to structure your time with the group. You are not required to be a teacher, but rather a facilitator to help the members in your group share their own insights and discoveries openly.

As you've read in the *Preface* and *How To Use This Guide* (at the beginning of this Workbook) each week has been divided into two sections:

1. The Study Guide as *information* to help you learn the concepts, and
2. The Journal as *interaction* to help you put the concepts into practice.

We suggest that in your weekly meeting, however, you reverse the order by briefly reviewing the Journal materials first, and then plunging into the Study Guide materials. The reason for this is that the *mechanics* of the diet is likely to be on everyone's mind first. This is particularly true in the first five weeks. After the fifth week, people will continue to keep a personal Journal for their own records, until the final week when they will again be asked to share their Journal entries with the group. During those first five weekly meetings, your job will be to ask people to share their Journal entries out loud with the group. You will need to move things along as the facilitator and be sure everyone who wishes has a turn to speak.

Then, you will spend the majority of your meeting time reviewing the Study Guide. As you will see, the Study Guide contains several exercises requiring readers to answer questions based on that week's reading assignment. Your job in the group meeting will be to ask individuals to *first* read the question aloud and *then* provide their answer. For example Week 1, Fact-Finder question 1:

Question:

1. Through what route of research did Dr. T. Colin Campbell come to the similar conclusions as Dr. George Malkmus?

Answer:

1. By walking a path paved by scientific investigation.

The answers to the questions are given on the following pages. As a rule, the answers to the Fact-Finder questions are specific, but the answers to the Points to Ponder are more subjective and personalized. In both cases, you will want to be sensitive to your group's willingness to discuss the answers along the way. You should consider *group discussion* to be the greatest goal, and should allow time for it whenever possible. You'll soon get a feeling for how to manage your time as the group leader. Keep one eye on the clock to decide when to stop the exercises and move into the closing prayer. Ideally, you'll want to allow enough time for the group take turns reading aloud the *Highlights from Reading*, before the closing prayer. This is also a good way to open up the group to further discussion, in case you've covered all the exercises earlier than expected.

Although I encourage you to close each meeting with a prayer, it is up to you and the group to decide the most comfortable way to proceed. Some ideas for *Prayer & Reflection* are provided to help you get started.

WEEK 1

JOURNAL
Day One: Your Dietary "Before Picture"

This exercise helps people become consciously aware of their current eating habits. If anyone expresses confusion about the meaning of *SAD foods*, *Living foods*, and *Hallelujah Cooked foods*, this is a good time to discuss those concepts briefly. Assure everyone that they will get a much better idea of those definitions in coming weeks. You should acknowledge people's reservations, but suggest everyone please reserve judgments for future weeks, after they have learned more.

Fact-Finder Answers

1. A path paved by scientific investigation

2. No

3. Life, diet and health

4. Carrot juice, celery, cucumber, leafy green vegetables

5. Genesis 1:29

6. Pulse and water

7. Age of Enlightenment

8. D) No classes

9. Standard American Diet

Points to Ponder

1. Ideas to discuss here might include conflicts of interest between humanitarian motives and profit motives in scientific research. Some may be led to discuss the concept of Intelligent

Design, as it relates to our Creator's provisions for health and nutrition.

2. Almost everyone can, if they think hard enough, come up with a time when circumstances combine in such a way that, upon reflection, we know God had a hand in the conclusion.

3. Not everyone will have examples; however, some people will have dramatic testimony.

4. Smoking is one obvious answer here; your group will think of others.

Highlights from Reading

Ask people to take turns reading aloud from this week's reading assignments. Time permitting, open up these points for discussion.

Prayer & Reflection

Close the meeting with a prayer. We have provided some suggestions for things to pray about, and people in your group may have special prayer requests. You might assign one person to lead the prayer, or open it up as a group prayer, as you see fit.

WEEK 2

JOURNAL
Choices and Goals

This is one of the most important weeks to discuss Journal entries. Encourage people to read aloud their complete set of Obstacles, Consequences, Goals, and Reasons. Try to keep things moving along, in order for everyone who wishes to have a turn, without getting bogged down. This will be a time when members in your group will reveal things they may have not discussed openly before, so you will need to be sensitive about that. You might stress here that by writing down goals and saying them out loud, we are actually taking a huge step to making them become real, by moving them from our unconscious to our conscious mind. God created the universe with the Word, and we follow His example by creating our new healthy condition with our spoken words.

Fact-Finder Questions

    1. Colon cancer

    2. C) evangelist

    3. C) Hallelujah!

    4. About 1,500 a day

    5. Fatty foods such as meats, dairy, and fried foods

    6. D) All of the above

    7. D) All of the above

    8. She knew she needed her lymph nodes for her immune system to function properly

    9. Sugar, white flour, meats, and processed foods

10. D) Trusting God and being obedient to His natural laws

Points to Ponder

1. Common answers and reactions to this question include everything from steaks to ice cream in terms of favorite foods, but often will also bring up fears about jeopardizing friendships and "normal" social events centered on eating.

2. It is very often the prospect of death or disability that finally motivates people to change destructive lifestyles; however, we are often concerned for the health and well-being of loved ones too. Discuss issues surrounding death or disability, which not only affects the afflicted person, but also his/her family. Death or disability of a bread-winner means loss of income; death of a parent means loss of a source of love and wisdom for a child. Think about the bride whose father won't walk her down the aisle, of the grandchild who won't have a grandparent to "spoil" him.

3. People here may wish to share small or large health problems that have already become obstacles to living a full life.

Highlights from Reading

Ask people to take turns reading aloud from this week's reading assignments. Time permitting, open up these points for discussion.

Prayer & Reflection

Close the meeting with a prayer. We have provided some suggestions for things to pray about, and people in your group may have special prayer requests. You might assign one person to lead the prayer, or open it up as a group prayer, as you see fit.

WEEK 3

JOURNAL

Give each group member an opportunity to share whether they have decided to follow the "Recovery" or "Maintenance" programs. If it seems natural, ask why they chose the path they did.

NOTE: You can mention to the group that the "Agreement with Myself" is a common technique used to help participants take seriously the time and fellowship they've invested with the group. As a group leader, you should urge everyone to fill out and sign the contract for his or her own benefit. This agreement is for the individual's use, and needn't be shared.

Fact-Finder Questions

1. Grass, herb (vegetables), seed, fruit, seed, good

2. Psalm 139:14: *"I will praise thee; for I am fearfully and wonderfully made; marvelous are thy works; and that my soul knoweth right well."*

3. E) All of the above

4. Body odor, acid stomach problems, Irritable Bowel Syndrome (IBS), colitis, ulcerated colitis, Crohn's disease, colon cancer

5. 912 years

6. Sugar

7. D) the Holy Spirit

8. Health

Points to Ponder

1. Read aloud Romans 7:14-20. In answer to the first question about people's bad habits, in spite of knowing better, we might hear about smoking, drinking, drugs, or sexual addiction. People may or may not want to share their "guilty pleasures," regarding food; however, common answers to this question are; coffee, sodas, candy, cakes, cookies, fried foods, fast foods and other junk foods.

2. People are confronted with Babylonian-type temptations all the time in our society, requiring people to resist temptations. Some answers may be:

Movies and TV. Hollywood is sometimes called "Hollywood Babylon" because of its explicit presentation of sex, immorality, and general indulgence.

Madison Avenue preys upon people's base instincts when advertising junk food, extravagant lifestyles, and sexually-oriented messages.

Popular music is a subtle way of presenting messages that are often filled with unseemly lyrics.

3. Common responses to this commentary are:

Sweet tastes in fruit: substituted with refined sugar or corn syrup in *candy, cakes, cookies, ice cream, sodas, and other foods not normally sweetened by nature.*

Fruity flavors and aromas: substituted with artificial flavors in *candy, gum, beverages, bottled flavors for baking, and even household products.*

Vibrant colors in fruits and vegetables: substituted with artificial colors in *canned (and even fresh) fruits and vegetables, processed foods of all kinds, candies, crackers, cereals, sodas, ice cream, and other snack foods.*

Crunchy textures of natural produce: substituted with *crackers, toasted breakfast cereals, chips, candies, and other snack foods.*

Luscious oils in nuts, seeds, avocados, and similar items: substituted with *hydrogenated oils in crackers, chips, snack foods, artificial cheese spreads, and practically every kind of processed food.*

Highlights from Reading

Ask people to take turns reading aloud from this week's reading assignments. Time permitting, open up these points for discussion.

Prayer & Reflection

Close the meeting with a prayer. We have provided some suggestions for things to pray about, and people in your group may have special prayer requests. You might assign one person to lead the prayer, or open it up as a group prayer, as you see fit.

Week 4

Journal

This was the week everyone read about the Hallelujah Diet explained. Today would be very good to ask people if they have a basic understanding about the difference between the three categories: A) Bad and SAD foods, B) Hallelujah Living Foods, and C) Hallelujah Cooked foods. Give members in the group an opportunity to explain the definitions openly. Then, with a show of hands, ask people if they feel this will be easy or hard for them. Ask them to remind each other aloud why they are doing this program, and if they think the rewards will outweigh the initial difficulties.

Fact-Finder Questions

1. 3 John 2 says, *"Beloved, I wish above all things that thou mayest prosper and be in **health**, even as thy soul prospereth."*

2. 300 times, physical

3. The increase in obesity

4. A) true; B) false; C) true; D) true; E) false

5. Weight gain

6. Heart attack

7. Exercise, lose weight, and eat right

Points to Ponder

1. Interesting point! Common responses to this might be:
Humans often place themselves as "gods," thinking they can create life, thereby jeopardizing their position in God's Kingdom, as lucifer did in the beginning.

Scientists really have no foundational concept of what *life* really is, because spiritual reality cannot be tested in controlled experimental conditions.

2. Many people find the idea that the aging process can be slowed by changes to diet is fantasy, yet countless stories you read in the book back it up. If you need to trigger a discussion, ask the class about what they think happens in cases of diabetes they read about, when patients cut meat and saturated fat from their diet.

3. Answers might include concepts like; people don't want to be responsible for themselves, if at all possible; or, humans seek the easy way out of problems whenever they can; or, people prefer comfort over discomfort, so the prospect of a "silver bullet drug" is an easier solution to swallow than having to do without one's comfort foods.

Highlights from Reading

Ask people to take turns reading aloud from this week's reading assignments. Time permitting, open up these points for discussion.

Prayer & Reflection

Close the meeting with a prayer. We have provided some suggestions for things to pray about, and people in your group may have special prayer requests. You might assign one person to lead the prayer, or open it up as a group prayer, as you see fit.

WEEK 5

JOURNAL

Discuss the Replacement Transition Journal, and go around the class give anyone who wishes an opportunity to share the choices they've made in their chart.

Fact-Finder Questions

1. It all belongs to God

2. D) A healthy plant-based diet filled with natural fiber

3. We rarely see any real turnaround—or repentance—from the lifestyle habits that cause illnesses in the first place

4. 225,000 people

5. 106,000

6. Immune system

7. A) Drugs; B) Radiation; C) Surgery

8. E) None of the above; they are equally unhealthy

Points to Ponder

1. Discuss any cases people wish to share on this subject, either about themselves or someone they know whose mission has been cut short due to poor health.

2. This is really another spin on the age old question: "If God is in charge of this world (our lives, the universe, etc.) then why does He allow things like war, suffering, corruption and the like?" This could lead to discussions including the topics of free will, temptation, steadfastness, and discernment. Sample response: God gave us free will and a world of options, but the

key to wise choices is to discern whether our choices and actions showing love toward other people.

3. This might be a good time for the group to share any additional misgivings as they encourage each other to move forward. Group leaders can get the ball rolling by expressing their own personal or family concerns.

Highlights from Reading

Ask people to take turns reading aloud from this week's reading assignments. Time permitting, open up these points for discussion.

Prayer & Reflection

Close the meeting with a prayer. We have provided some suggestions for things to pray about, and people in your group may have special prayer requests. You might assign one person to lead the prayer, or open it up as a group prayer, as you see fit.

WEEK 6

JOURNAL

Remind people this is a "Journey" to good health that they are sharing, and their Journals can be helpful not only to themselves, but to each other. Share and discuss anyone's progress, insights, experiences, or difficulties with the previous week's food choices. Give members in the group an opportunity to discuss openly their feelings of excitement and/or frustration about this journey. You can open the discussion by asking if anyone wants to refer to this week's Journal entries of three categories: A) Bad and SAD foods, B) Hallelujah Living Foods, and C) Hallelujah Cooked foods.

Fact-Finder Questions

1. Living food

2. G) All of the above; additionally, water content is lost and fiber loses its benefit

3. Disease, low vitality, loss of quality of life, loss of spiritual and mental clarity, and early death

4. B) Active enzymes

5. 107 degrees

6. They began to get sick and die

7. A) Stop doing what caused the problems in the first place; and B) Rush the proper supplies of micronutrients to the cells of the body so they can accomplish their job of self-repair

8. A) Claws and teeth (sharp with no flat molars); B) Acidic saliva; C) Stomach acidity (twenty times more powerful than herbivores); D) Length of intestinal tract (relatively short compared to herbivores); E) Intestinal shape (smooth—no bumps or pockets). There are many other traits that would also be correct answers.

9. False: Raw vegetables is the correct answer

Points to Ponder

1. Go around the group, or ask for volunteers to share their answers. Typical dead foods would be burgers, fries, pizza, or anything cooked. Living foods would be salads, slaws, smoothies, veggie sandwiches, raw fruits, vegetables, nuts, or seeds.

2. Possible answers here might be:

People adapted for survival during times when there was no available produce.

Once started eating meat, the habit becomes self-perpetuating.

Affluence encourages people to buy the most expensive food source they can afford, which long ago was reserved for kings, but is now available to those with moderate incomes.

3. An open discussion regarding the stumbling blocks that group members have encountered already as they transition to the full Hallelujah Diet will be instructive and encouraging, particularly to those who feel as if others in the group are having early success while they continue to struggle inwardly or within their family group. Ask people to share openly the ups and downs of their journey.

Highlights from Reading

Ask people to take turns reading aloud from this week's reading assignments. Time permitting, open up these points for discussion.

Prayer & Reflection

Close the meeting with a prayer. We have provided some suggestions for things to pray about, and people in your group may have special prayer requests. You might assign one person to lead the prayer, or open it up as a group prayer, as you see fit.

WEEK 7

JOURNAL

Remind people this is a "Journey" to good health they are sharing, and their Journals can be helpful not only to themselves, but to each other. Share and discuss anyone's progress, insights, experiences, or difficulties with the previous week's food choices. Give members in the group an opportunity to openly discuss their feelings of excitement and/or frustration about their journey. You can begin the discussion by asking if anyone wants to refer to this week's Journal entries of three categories: A) Bad and SAD foods, B) Hallelujah Living Foods, and C) Hallelujah Cooked foods.

Fact-Finder Questions

1. A) Cooking meat destroys enzymes needed for digestion; B) Protein content far exceeds human needs; C) Diseased meat in mass-produced food supply; D) seafood polluted with toxins

2. Answers: B and D

3. 100 pounds

4. Bacteria, antibiotics, and growth hormones

5. Animal products

6. 34 percent

7. TRUE or FALSE
    A) T
    B) T
    C) T

8. Headache, nausea, rashes, pimples, coughing up "crud," diarrhea or constipation

Points to Ponder

1. This could spark some fun conversations in the group. Ask if anyone has ever hunted for survival, as spelled out in the lesson question. If anyone is still having trouble giving up meat, consider recent books such as:

Mad Cowboy by Howard Lyman.

Slaughterhouse: The Shocking Story of Greed, Neglect, and Inhumane Treatment Inside the U.S. Meat Industry by Gail A. Eisnitz.

2. Possible triggers that could cause individuals to become aware of the link between eating animal products and bad health might be:

National awareness of those dangers, through media campaigns similar to the anti-tobacco campaigns by the American Cancer Society.

Warning labels by the U.S. Surgeon General.

Examples set by respected celebrities or public figures who are proponents of vegetarianism.

3. Have the group discuss any symptoms they are experiencing that might be attributed to detox. It always helps when you realize you're not the only one feeling like this!

Highlights from Reading

Ask people to take turns reading aloud from this week's reading assignments. Time permitting, open up these points for discussion.

Prayer & Reflection

Close the meeting with a prayer. We have provided some suggestions for things to pray about, and people in your group may have special prayer requests. You might assign one person to lead the prayer, or open it up as a group prayer, as you see fit.

WEEK 8

JOURNAL

Remind people this is a "Journey" to good health they are sharing, and their Journals can be helpful not only to themselves, but to each other. Share and discuss anyone's progress, insights, experiences, or difficulties with the previous week's food choices. Give members in the group an opportunity to openly discuss their feelings of excitement and/or frustration about their journey. Begin the discussion by asking if anyone wants to refer to this week's Journal entries of three categories: A) Bad and SAD foods, B) Hallelujah Living Foods, and C) Hallelujah Cooked foods.

Fact-Finder Questions

1. D) To extend shelf life

2. Immune system; one full day

3. A) True; B) False; C) True; D) True

4. E) All of the above

5. Possible answers include bacteria, toxins, microbes, cancers cells, viruses, and parasites

6. A) False; B) False; C) False

7. B) Artificially sweetened soda

8. Paste or glue

9. Acidity

Points to Ponder

1. Aside from the obvious answer—that parents should simply feed their children a healthy diet (and adhere to one

themselves)—there are interesting points to discuss here regarding the role of government in the public health. Think about the warning labels on cigarettes—have they helped?

2. The group leader hopes that participants don't have a lot to contribute to this list; however, remember to encourage rather than judge!

3. This should be a fun exercise to keep group members motivated. Pass blank papers and pencils to the group, asking them to draft the message to the commander back at headquarters. Then read the messages aloud, with feeling!

Highlights from Reading

Ask people to take turns reading aloud from this week's reading assignments. Time permitting, open up these points for discussion.

Prayer & Reflection

Close the meeting with a prayer. We have provided some suggestions for things to pray about, and people in your group may have special prayer requests. You might assign one person to lead the prayer, or open it up as a group prayer, as you see fit.

WEEK 9

JOURNAL

Remind people this is a "Journey" to good health they are sharing, and their Journals can be helpful not only to themselves, but to each other. Share and discuss anyone's progress, insights, experiences, or difficulties with the previous week's food choices. Give members in the group an opportunity to openly discuss their feelings of excitement and/or frustration about their journey. You can begin the discussion by asking if anyone wants to refer to this week's Journal entries of three categories: A) Bad and SAD foods, B) Hallelujah Living Foods, and C) Hallelujah Cooked foods.

Fact-Finder Questions

1. The 1996 USDA Food Pyramid showed that we should eat 6 to 11 servings of bread, cereal, rice, and pasta everyday. It noted nothing about whole grain, brown rice, or whole-wheat pasta. It recommended fruits and vegetables but didn't specify dead or living food. And it actually listed such deadly items as sweets, margarine, sugars, soft drinks, candies, and sweet desserts. The 2005 USDA MyPyramid has some modifications. For one thing, it suggests exercise, which is a noticeable improvement. There are no serving suggestions but they have eliminated sweets, colas, and desserts from the suggested foods.

2. F) All of the above

3. Slower metabolic function; digestion problems; constipation; formation of diseases; low vitality; loss of quality of life; loss of spiritual and mental clarity; early death

4. A) False; B) True; C) False; D) True

5. Through juicing

6. A) Sugary foods; B) Caffeine; C) Alcohol

7. Prescription drugs

Points to Ponder

1. It will be affirming for members of the group—particularly if they are of a certain age—to discuss this with others; while the information pointing to good health was available to researchers and scholars, it may not have been as readily available to the general public in those times. In fact, as we have seen, the general public was being duped. Still, some may point to grandparents or "health nuts" whom they remember advocating, "eat your vegetables!"

2. Use a match to light a candle in front of the class. Then ask for a volunteer to blow the candle out. Ask the volunteer to then relight it, without using another flame, but using only the "dead" match. Of course, it can't be done. Ask the class to discuss the comparison about how only life can perpetuate life, and can't be maintained by eating dead food.

3. This might be an exercise in which people close their eyes and listen one person reading the scene aloud. Or it may be done as a silent exercise from which the Group Leader goes directly into the closing prayer.

Highlights from Reading

Ask people to take turns reading aloud from this week's reading assignments. Time permitting, open up these points for discussion.

Prayer & Reflection

Close the meeting with a prayer. We have provided some suggestions for things to pray about, and people in your group may have special prayer requests. You might assign one person to lead the prayer, or open it up as a group prayer, as you see fit.

WEEK 10

JOURNAL

Remind people this is a "Journey" to good health they are sharing, and their Journals can be helpful not only to themselves, but to each other. Share and discuss anyone's progress, insights, experiences, or difficulties with the previous week's food choices. Give members in the group an opportunity to openly discuss their feelings of excitement and/or frustration about their journey. You can begin the discussion by asking if anyone wants to refer to this week's Journal entries of three categories: A) Bad and SAD foods, B) Hallelujah Living Foods, and C) Hallelujah Cooked foods.

Fact-Finder Questions

1. A) False; B) True; C) True; D) False; E) True

2. Cardiovascular exercise, flexibility routines, and strength training

3. The brain

4. No

5. As good health feels!

6. C)

7. The ambitions of the mind with the limitations of the body

8. D) All of the above

Points to Ponder

1. There are two questions here, and Group Leaders can start the ball rolling with suggestions for answers to the first, such as work-related issues, commuting (road rage), or family

relationship problems. The group members may well have many more they wish to share. The second half of the discussion—ways to dissipate stress—could be very informative for some participants who need help finding time for exercise in their schedules.

2. Comfort foods is a subject that always sparks a myriad of memories and lively discussions. Group leaders would be advised to focus on the last part of this point, connecting emotional ties to named comfort foods.

Highlights from Reading

Ask people to take turns reading aloud from this week's reading assignments. Time permitting, open up these points for discussion.

Prayer & Reflection

Close the meeting with a prayer. We have provided some suggestions for things to pray about, and people in your group may have special prayer requests. You might assign one person to lead the prayer, or open it up as a group prayer, as you see fit.

WEEK 11

JOURNAL

Time to bring up the Potluck meal plan as described in this week's Journal exercise. As the leader, you can either serve as the coordinator of the event, or else assign that job to someone in the group. Don't leave the meeting today until you have nailed down the time and place where the Potluck will be held. Also, prepare everyone to share their "After Picture" with the group, if they are willing.

Remind people this is a "Journey" to good health they are sharing, and their Journals can be helpful not only to themselves, but to each other. Share and discuss anyone's progress, insights, experiences, or difficulties with the previous week's food choices. Give members in the group an opportunity to openly discuss their feelings of excitement and/or frustration about their journey. You can begin the discussion by asking if anyone wants to refer to this week's Journal entries of three categories: A) Bad and SAD foods, B) Hallelujah Living Foods, and C) Hallelujah Cooked foods.

Fact-Finder Questions

1. The healing crisis

2. A) Skin; B) Lungs; C) Colon; D) Kidneys; E) Sinuses

3. A) False; B) True; C) False; D) True

4. Chlorine and fluoride

5. Oxygen starvation of the brain

6. Vegetables and fruits

7. Melanin

8. Dehydrated and have skin that is congested and toxic

Points to Ponder

1. The group might want to consider withdrawal from sugar, caffeine, nicotine, or other substances. Ask people to talk about the withdrawal symptoms they have personally experienced when going cold turkey from those substances.

2. It may be relatively easy to achieve this in midsummer; the group might want to discuss how seasonal changes will require flexibility and creativity.

3. This could be an excellent refresher course in human relations. Think outside the animal cracker box! Set a little role—playing scenario, taking turns to be the parent or grandparent. The value here is to think ahead about how to respond to real life situations, maintaining a loving, nonjudgmental and Christ-like attitude.

Highlights from Reading

Ask people to take turns reading aloud from this week's reading assignments. Time permitting, open up these points for discussion.

Prayer & Reflection

Close the meeting with a prayer. We have provided some suggestions for things to pray about, and people in your group may have special prayer requests. You might assign one person to lead the prayer, or open it up as a group prayer, as you see fit.

WEEK 12

JOURNAL

This is the final week of the program, and time for any and all who want to share their "After Picture" with the group. Some groups might choose to do this at the Potluck meal. We at Hallelujah Acres greatly encourage you to combine these two activities—it is great fun, and very eye-opening.

Results in the "After Picture" may be dramatic for some and not for others. There might be a mixture of emotions ranging from elation to embarrassment (depending on how committed individual members were to the program), but it is good for the group to share their experiences, and to be supportive to one another. Let everyone know that the group is grateful to them for just hanging in there, doing the work, and coming to all the meetings.

Please convey our congratulations to the group from Hallelujah Acres, and especially to you for keeping the sessions moving smoothly over the past three months.

Fact-Finder Questions

1. By consuming a lifetime of salt, pepper, flavor enhancers, and other additives

2. They deaden our taste buds to the real tastes in natural foods

3. Dying and replacing themselves at approximately 300 million cells per minute

4. Approximately one year

5. Two weeks

6. Eating more volume of the *highest nutrient-containing* foods on the planet. The greatest anticancer foods should be the foundation of your diet

7. Addictive cravings, making us want to overeat

8. We should work first on becoming healthy

Points to Ponder

1. Go around the room and have everyone read his or her speech. A sample might be: "It's OK, Marcia; I understand your resistance to trying new things. After all, this tastes different from anything you've ever tried before! But it's so good for you! And after a few weeks when you start to see the wonderful changes in your health that come as a result of trying these healthy new foods, you'll consume them with enthusiasm and gratitude. I promise!"

2. It is an interesting paradox that in the wealthiest nation on earth we have the most malnourished citizenry. Ask people to confess the foods they just can't get enough of—it might be surprising. Typical answers might be peanuts, potato chips, chocolate. But some people get really hooked on Big Macs, pizza, lattes, and other things that don't provide any nutrition.

3. It is common to encounter resistance when espousing uncommon ideas. The group may want to share ways that each has used to discuss his or her new lifestyle with friends and family. In the end, the best way to influence anyone to adopt a new lifestyle is to set a good example. Discuss ways in which you can do that: what you eat for lunch; which restaurant you suggest; what you politely decline to eat when offered.

Highlights from Reading

Ask people to take turns reading aloud from this week's reading assignments. Time permitting, open up these points for discussion.

Prayer & Reflection

Close the meeting with a prayer. We have provided some suggestions for things to pray about, and people in your group may have special prayer requests. You might assign one person to lead the prayer, or open it up as a group prayer, as you see fit.

Additional copies of this book and other
book titles from DESTINY IMAGE are
available at your local bookstore.

For a complete list of our titles,
visit us at www.destinyimage.com
Send a request for a catalog to:

Destiny Image® Publishers, Inc.
P.O. Box 310
Shippensburg, PA 17257-0310

*"Speaking to the Purposes of God for this
Generation and for the Generations to Come."*